AF548608

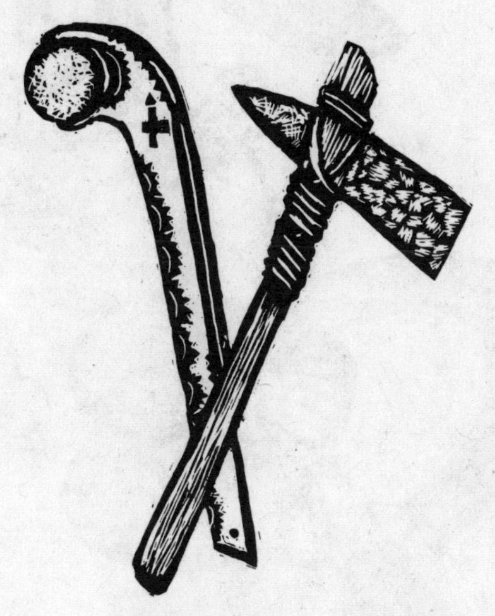

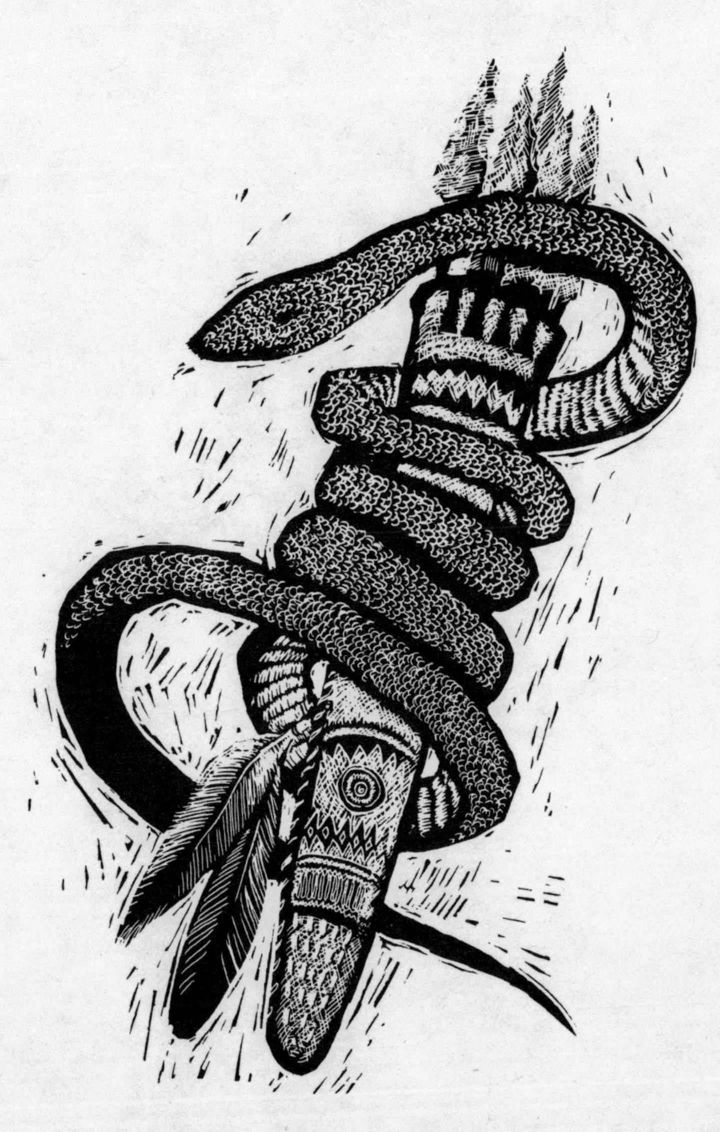

FIRST ENCOUNTER SERIES

The INDIAN and the WHITE MAN in Massachusetts & Rhode Island

Chandler Whipple

THE BERKSHIRE TRAVELLER PRESS
Stockbridge, Massachusetts 01262

First Encounter Series

The Indian and White Man in Connecticut

The Indian and White Man in Massachusetts and Rhode Island

The Indian and White Man in Maine (forthcoming)

The Indian and White Man in Vermont and New Hampshire (forthcoming)

Illustrations and cover by
Janice T. Lindstrom

First Printing

Whipple, Chandler.
First Encounter Series

Summary: A history of the Indians in Massachusetts and Rhode Island, describing their way of life and customs from their first appearance in the area to the present day, emphasizing the changes forced upon them by the white man.

1. Indians of North America—New England. 2. Indians of North America—Massachusetts. 3. Indians of North America—Rhode Island. [1. Indians of North America—New England. 2. Indians of North America—Massachusetts. 3. Indians of North America—Rhode Island] I. Lindstrom, Janice, illus. II. Title.

E78.N5W45 970.4'44 73-93961 ISBN 0-912944-12-9

ACKNOWLEDGEMENTS

My thanks go first of all to Frank (Wamsutta), President of the Federation of Eastern Indians League, and his wife Priscilla, of West Chatham, who provided me with a great deal of information early in my researches and increased my enthusiasm to continue my efforts. Princess White Flower (Zara Ciscoe Brough) of the Hassanamisco Reservation went to considerable trouble to answer many questions for which I had found no answers, particularly concerning the Nipmuck Indians. And in the beginning, it was Mrs. Polly Pierce, Curator of the excellent Historical Collection of the Stockbridge, Massachusetts, Library who got me on the right road.

Mr. Kenneth Mynter of Claverack, New York, amateur archaeologist and researcher of Indian lore, also deserves my thanks for filling me in on certain matters, as does Mr. Edmund Swigart of the Shepaug Valley Archaeological Society, Inc., of Washington, Connecticut.

And my thanks to Mrs. Nancy O'Reilly of *The Berkshire Traveller Press,* for her helpful suggestions and editing of the manuscript.

I also found useful information in *The Southern New England Indians to 1725,* the 1935 doctorial thesis of Robert Austin Warner, the original of which is in the Yale University Library.

The concluding quotation on page 30 is from the Paiute song, *The Grass on the Mountain,* which was translated by the late Mary Austin. I found this in *An Anthology of World Poetry,* edited by Mark Van Doren, first published in 1928 and recently republished by Harcourt, Brace & Jovanovich. It first appeared in the translator's *The American Rhythm,* and I am grateful to late Professor Van Doren for clearing up for me the matter of publishing rights on this bit of verse.

Chandler Whipple

CONTENTS

What is already known and believed about the origin of man in America has recently been catapulted into a deep dilemma by new findings uncovered in an ancient Mexican stream bed. For decades, archaeological and geological studies have shown that man first migrated into the Western Hemisphere about 40,000 years ago over the then-existing land bridge between Alaska and Siberia and became the native inhabitant-which we call the Indian.

Prior to that time there has been no generally accepted evidence of the existence of man in the New World. However, a team of geologists has now unearthed advanced stone tools at a site near Pueblo, Mexico, which they have dated, through various technological methods, as far back as 250,000 years! Furthermore, these tools were more sophisticated than those appearing in Europe and Asia 200,000 years later. The evidence appears to be geologically sound, but is in direct conflict with all known archaeological data. According to one of the geologists, "At present, an impasse exists."

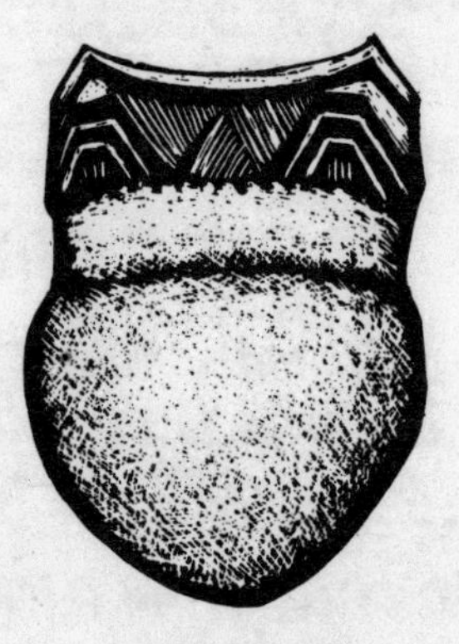

THE WOODLAND PEOPLE

Although we are confronted with an unsolved anthropological mystery, we must realize that there are now close to one million Indians in the United States, and many million non-Indian Americans who still know little to nothing about them. Doubtless even more have never met an Indian face to face, or recognized him if they did. They would probably have expected to see a red man, whereas the Indian is not red, unless he has painted his face red for a ceremonial occasion. But a pure-blooded Indian can be just about any other shade from dark brown to very nearly white.

Nor does he always have the high cheekbones, broad face and flattish nose of the Mongolian. Often he does, but he may even have an aquiline nose and narrow face. Usually his hair is black and straight, but there are Indians with lighter hair, and with wavy hair. There are Indians who are short and squat, and Indians who are tall and lean. In short, like the rest of us, Indians come in all shapes and sizes.

The one thing we can say definitely is that the Indian is the earliest human inhabitant of the American continents. He did not write down his history to prove this. He only handed down his legends around the campfire, and occasionally in a sort of written sign language.

But we do have radio-carbon dating, and this, along with the extensive researches of anthropologists and archaeologists, makes it possible to state with reasonable assurance that when some of the forebears of the Indian crossed over from Siberia into Alaska, they had already discovered fire. They also had domesticated the dog, and presumably they were hunters, following game such as the wooly mamoth, which was then present in both Siberia and North America. They would have been followed by other hunters, and gradually these early arrivals worked their way southward, down the Mackenzie Valley and other ice-free corridors, thus over the centuries reaching the United States and Mexico. They may also have gone on to South America, but as archaeologist Louis A. Brennan points out, radio-carbon dating shows Indians to the south, and even in New Mexico, before the melting of the Wisconsin glacier had opened a passageway from Alaska. This leaves us with an unresolved puzzle, but the recent voyages of Thor Heyerdahl and others across the Pacific on rafts offer a sound argument for the possibility that some of these early Indians may have come by sea across the Pacific.

In any case, it appears quite certain that the Indian is principally of Mongoloid stock, possibly mixed with some Caucasoid. It may even be, as some scholars have suggested, that at the time the Indian came to America these two of the so-called Races of Man had not yet sharply divided into separate races. If that is true, then we could even go further and say that the Indian makes up a race of his own.

He should then have a name of his own, rather than the one mistakenly fastened upon him by Columbus. He does not, because there was no language common to all Indians, When the white man came to America, he found literally hundreds of tribes and smaller groups, each speaking a different tongue or dialect, usually not understandable to the others. Language experts have detected certain root words and sounds common to large numbers of tribes, and by this method have determined to their satisfaction that the Indians of the United States and Canada can be separated into six different groups or linguistic stocks. These are the Algonkian or Algonkian-Washakian, the Hokan-Sioux, the Penutian, the Nadene or Athabascan, the Eskimo-Aleut, and the Aztec-Tanoan or Uto-Aztecan.

The Eskimo-Aleut group lived and still lives on the shores of Alaska and Canada, in Greenland and Siberia. It may have been the last of the Indian groups to cross from Asia. The Athabascan family occupied most of northwest Canada and Alaska, principally inland, although they also lived along the western coasts of both these lands, while a large group were in our Southwest and a few along the West

Coast. The Penutian stock also lived along the West Coast, from just below Puget Sound southward through what are now the states of Washington, Oregon, and California. Principally to the east of these and stretching southward into Mexico was the Uto-Aztecan group.

From well into central Canada, sweeping southward through the Great Plains down along the American Gulf Coast, and northward again to Lakes Erie and Ontario and beyond, were to be found the Hokan-Sioux. In an even greater sweep all across Canada from inland off the coast of Labrador to Puget Sound, then southward through Minnesota, Wisconsin and Michigan, and northward along the Atlantic Coast from Cape Hatteras to the Gulf of St. Lawrence, lived the great Algonkian family.

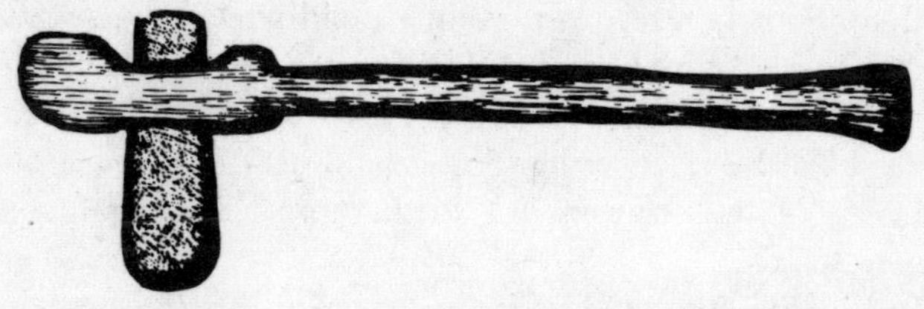

The Algonkian group thus included all the tribes of New England, with the exception of a few Mohawks (Hokan-Sioux) who lived, at least for a time, along the western and northern borders of Vermont. To the north of the Atlantic Coast group were the Algonkian hunters of Canada, while the Algonkian to the west, around the Great Lakes and down the Mississippi Valley, were growers of corn.

Since the Indians of New England both hunted and grew corn, one cannot be certain whether they came originally from the west or down from the north to spread along the coast, but the former now appears more probable. If so, the art of growing Indian corn could have come to them from the Hopewell Indians, the Moundbuilders of the Midwest. There does appear to have been a relationship between the Algonkians and some of that long since vanished group, perhaps through the Delaware (Lenni Lenape), also an Algonkian tribe. Some New England Indians even spoke of the Delaware as their "grandfathers" but this could have been only legend.

Where and How They Lived

These Indians were not a nomadic people. They lived in small villages, generally of not more than a hundred people, in domed wigwams *(wetus)* usually made of elm bark stretched over pole frames. The cone-shaped tipi belonged to the Indians of the western plains, although the Penobscot of Maine did have a birchbark tipi which resembled it. The frames of the wigwams consisted of saplings, thin and green, which were bent into a half-circle and the ends planted in the ground. More saplings were bent to go around these frames in a horizontal circle, with all lashed together at the crossings. The covering was then tied into the frames, leaving a smoke-hole at the top and a small entrance at the bottom. Sometimes skins of animals and woven grasses were added to the elm bark for further protection, and in the north where birch was plentiful, the bark of that tree usually formed the basic covering. Sods could also be piled around the base of the wigwam for further protection against the winter winds.

Inside, the hut could be quite cozy, for in the center, in a pit lined with stones, the occupants kept a small fire burning. Around the walls often stood crude shelves or benches, made of poles and covered with furs, for resting and sleeping. This type of bed became even more common after the coming of the white man made boards available. Lacking it, they slept upon the ground, on mats or fur robes, with their feet toward the fire.

The wigwams were usually small, of family size, but the larger ones could sleep eight to ten families. The River Indians of Connecticut are said to have constructed some as much as sixty feet long, which would have resembled not so much a dome as a quonset hut. For the most part the huts and the village were their permanent home, and the villages usually stood beside a stream or upon the seashore. Sometimes they were stockaded, particularly if the village was the home of a great chief or sachem. Nearby the women planted corn and beans, tended their vegetable garden, and searched the surrounding country for nuts and berries.

In the surrounding area, the men hunted and fished. This

was considered man's work, for often they traveled many miles in search of game, and had to carry it back to the village.

Sometimes, if the planting ground had become exhausted or the hunting was not good, a whole village might pick up its scant belongings and move to a better location. Occasionally they also found it necessary to change location for sanitary reasons, but more often any move was only a seasonal one, such as going to the seashore for shellfish. In any case, they did not wander about as did the hunter Algonkians of Canada, who were true nomads.

Tools and Equipment

Their tools were crude by our standards. Until the white man came, they had no metal, with the occasional exception of copper. This would presumably have come down to them through trade from the Algonkian tribes of the upper Great Lakes region, and was hammered into ornaments. But they made axes and knives by chipping stone until it had an edge. The axes, or tomahawks, were then grooved at the small end by the same process, and a wooden handle affixed by splitting the wood at one end, fitting it around the grooves, and then lashing the ends together with reed or leather thongs. Stone bowls were hollowed out of one stone by grinding another stone against it for hours.

For the preparation, eating and storing of food the Algonkians of New England resorted to platters and large spoons carved out of wood. They also wove bags, mats and baskets from reeds and similar materials, and some of them made a crude unglazed black pottery. Since these utensils would not hold water, for cooking they used vessels made of birch or elm bark, sewed with thongs and sealed with pitch or spruce gum. Their hoe was often a clamshell tied to a stick.

Yet with such crude tools they could, in a few days, build a birchbark canoe. This involved stripping the bark from the tree and turning it inside out. Then it was shaped in a frame of poles planted in the ground. Next, with rootlets, the builders lashed the top to gunwales which met at either end and were tied together there. Thin strips of wood must also be laid inside the bark, endwise and athwartships, and bent saplings from gunwale to gunwale as bracing. All separate pieces were sewed together with thongs or plant fibers, and all seams glued with spruce gum and charcoal. The result was a craft so light, buoyant and sturdy that it still is a model for the canoes of the present day.

The birchbark canoe served as the swiftest means of travel for Indians as far south as northern Massachusetts. South of that, where the birch was less plentiful, heavier canoes were made of elm or other bark. The dugout was also common there. Making this required burning through a fallen tree at the proper length, stripping the bark from the trunk, then hollowing it by steady chipping with axes and knives, preferably after the wood had been rendered less tough by fire.

The more northerly Indians also made snowshoes and toboggans for winter travel. These, as well as the birchbark canoe, were Indian inventions.

APPEARANCE AND DRESS

The men of the New England Indians were generally tall, well-muscled and strong, while the women tended to be short. Most were quite light in color. The nose was usually aquiline, and the face appears to have been less broad than that of the western Indian. They were, in fact, "long-headed," like the Hopewell Indians. (The Adena Indians, who also constructed mounds and who appeared in the Midwest before the Hopewell group, are classified as "round-headed," and probably, according to Brennan, drifted up from Mexico or Central America.)

Their clothing was simple but sturdy. In summer, the men wore only a hide breechclout, or at most, trousers and leggins of skin, the women, a wrap-around skirt of the same material. To this they added soft-soled moccasins, often beautifully decorated. In winter or where the weather was colder, the Indian also added shirts and blouses, also of skin, along with fur robes and feather cloaks, the former usually decorated with porcupine quills, seashells and the like. In summer, children below the age of puberty normally went naked.

The women wore their hair loose or braided, and some of the men did the same. Warriors, however, often shaved or pulled out all the hair save a center roach, or scalplock, which ran from the forehead all the way down the back of the neck. They usually added bear grease to the hair to give it a shine, and thrust in decorations of feathers. They also greased their bodies—in the winter for warmth, in the summer to ward off insects. Some New England Indians were tattooed. The Indian had little body hair.

Many of the sachems also wore caps and aprons decorated with different colored beads, and sometimes belts made of wampum.

Foods and Cooking

When the hunting was good and the season good for growing, the Indians of New England had plenty of food and a varied diet. They grew the Indian or mixed corn, the Johnny-cake corn, and popcorn, as well as beans, squash and pumpkins. *Yokeag* or *nokechick,* which was yellow corn parched in hot ashes and pounded with stones into powder, proved an excellent food to carry on a long journey, for three teaspoonfuls were enough for a meal. Wild berries and mushrooms could be had for the picking, as could beech, hickory and chestnuts, as well as acorns and sunflower seeds. In the spring, they tapped the maple trees and boiled down the sap for sugar. Deer and beaver, along with wildfowl such as turkey and duck, and small game abounded in the

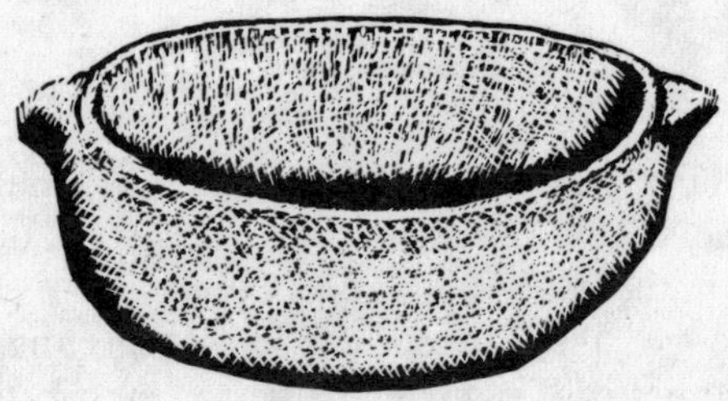

forest, to be hunted in the fall and winter. Fish and shellfish (clams and lobsters), even whales, could be found along the shore. But with only the means the Indians had for getting it, all this was not to be had easily. Fish might be caught in weirs, some animals in cunningly concealed traps. The Indian also used calls to bring the larger animals within range, but once there, the hunter had to depend upon the bow and arrow.

Mostly, to bring down a moose or deer required endless tracking and stalking. The Indian knew well the lore of the woods; boys learned it at an early age, and went out as children to bring back their first game. Even so, it was not always possible to bring back enough food for the entire village, and sometimes for days there was hunger in the wigwams.

Food, when not cooked over an open fire, usually was

"stone-boiled" in the birch or elm bark vessels already mentioned. That is to say, the women poured water into the vessels, followed by enough hot stones from the fire to bring it to a boil. Stone-boiling was practiced in particular by the more northerly of the New England Indians. Forked sticks were placed on either side of the fire, supporting a horizontal stick which suspended the cooking vessels over the flame.

Customs

The Indians had many customs which may seem strange to us, yet they made a great deal of sense in the light of their religious beliefs, the lives they led, the wars they waged. For example, they had special huts for the segregation of women during their menstrual periods. Their belief was that a woman, because of her ability to bear children, possessed special and mysterious powers. Related as menstruation was to the process of child-bearing, men feared that if they came near a woman at such a time, her power might be so great as to take away from a man his own special powers as a warrior and huntsman.

Another special hut, with room for a large fire, served as a sweat lodge, where the Algonkian could cleanse his pores for the purpose of religious purification.

An old and well known Indian custom not always understood by the European was the giving and receiving of presents. Among the Indians themselves, the man who gave generously was highly respected. When an Indian maiden agreed to become the bride of a young brave, gifts were sent by the young man's parents to hers, and her parents in turn sent presents to his. Gifts were given to the parents of a child at the time of its naming ceremony, and a good hunter was expected to give away part of the meat from his kill. A man who had killed another must give gifts to the dead man's relations to save his own life. A chief or sachem had to be wealthy by Indian standards, for if he wished to influence his people, he must be prepared to give presents upon many occasions. This made it necessary, particularly after the coming of white men introduced a greater variety of presents, for the sachem to receive the lion's share of these gifts made to his tribe or group.

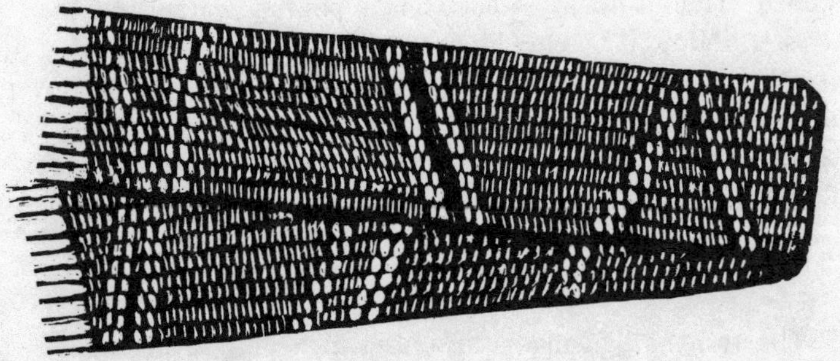

Up to this time, gifts had been fairly simple, and included beaver pelts, skins of animals, tobacco, bark, and ointment—as well as that most highly regarded gift of all, wampum. The white man brought in gifts that only he could offer, such as beaver hats trimmed with lace, blankets that were brightly colored, knives, bullet molds, war paint, metal pots, scissors, needles, and threads. These types of presents increased as French vied with English for the friendship and alliance in war of the Indian tribes.

Wampum had long been considered of great value for various reasons. For one thing, before the coming of the white man's tools it was very difficult to make. The white wampum was made from the inside of the conch shell, while the more valuable dark wampum—actually purple or dark blue—came from the shell of the quahog clam or the mussel. With stone tools these little tubular-shaped beads, seldom more than half an inch long, first had to be cut out of the shells, and then with such tools a tiny hole had to be bored through from end to end. Through the hole, very narrow strips of deerskin were then inserted to make strings, belts, bracelets, and other ornaments.

In addition, wampum had a mystic significance which cannot quite be explained today. A message in wampum literally "spoke louder than words." Properly designated, belts of wampum could carry the history of a tribe over the centuries. The presentation of a wampum belt could be a request for peace or a declaration of war.

Presents, and particularly presents of wampum, were a necessity at diplomatic councils held between friendly tribes or tribal groups. The greater the gift, the greater the attention lavished upon the speaker at the council. Wampum, while not regarded as money in the sense that the whites later caused it to be regarded, was still a medium of exchange, sometimes a tribute, or a ransom for a captive.

It should be added for the speaker at the council, however, that his words also carried weight. The Indians held a good speechmaker in high regard. A man who was not brave in war but spoke well and wisely in council might still be highly respected by his tribe.

When an Indian gave a present, he expected to receive a gift at least equal in value, or the return of his own gift. Thus the phrase, "Indian giving."

The smoking of the stone pipe also had great meaning. It could signify a peace or cement an alliance. So, of course, could "burying the hatchet" while "taking up the hatchet" would begin a war. Hatchets were sometimes ceremoniously buried when peace was made.

Religion

The Indian was a religious man, the Algonkian particularly so, for his religion embraced all the wonders about him: the rumble of thunder, the flash of lightning, the four winds, all things moving and all things growing, and even the earth he walked upon. His Great Spirit, known by some tribes as Kiehtan, was a distant but kindly being, who dwelt somewhere off to the southwest where the good Indian would go when he died. While he worshiped this spirit, and Manibozho who remade the world after the flood, he also worshiped in a sense all things about him, even the kindly animals who provided him food. He believed that these animals were gods of a sort who could change their shape at will into that of a man.

The Indians also worshiped, or rather made sacrifices to, various spirits of evil and mischief, such as Hobbamock, and this caused the Puritan Englishmen to consider them as devil worshipers. In a sense they were, because they feared the evil spirits and felt they must be appeased. Kiehtan, being a benevolent deity, did not seek appeasement, but

only good deeds. One legend tells that after he had made man, he was saddened because man would be aware of death. Hence he gave man tobacco for a solace. Thus tobacco, and the smoking of it, held a religious significance for the Indian. The same held true for *Kinnikinnick,* the mixture of bark and dried leaves, such as sumac and bearberry, which served as a substitute for the more northerly New England Indians who could not grow tobacco.

As children, most Algonkians fasted, seeking a vision. If the vision appeared, it would be in human form, but when it turned away, the child would see an animal or a bird. He was then expected to get a few hairs or feathers left by the vision, which became a sacred token to keep with him always and to which he gave offerings of tobacco smoke, seeking thus to call up his spirit power. A medicine man, shaman or *powwow,* as he has been variously called, must gain this vision—this supernatural help—but all men sought it, even girls up to the age of puberty. Nearly every act of the Indian required its ritual and prayer, from hunting game to killing it, from planting corn to plowing it, even taking of clay from the earth for pottery.

The medicine man or powwow was not truly a priest, in the sense that we think of such a man today, nor was he quite a doctor. He performed some of the duties of both and was somewhat of a magician or soothsayer as well. His healing function included the use of herb medicines plus a great deal of this magic and soothsaying.

Both of these methods of treatment were scorned as primitive savagery by the English physicians who first came to America, and whose own methods were primitive indeed. Yet today dozens of Indian herbal remedies are listed in the *United States Pharmacopeia,* official source book of medicinal products, and in one form or another are in medical use. And recently the value of the powwow's "magic and soothsaying" has been discovered by psychiatrists. Recently the U.S. Government financed a program whereby Navajo Indian medicine men taught younger tribesmen the ancient methods, described by a psychiatrist as "highly sophisticated psychosomatic medicine."

"Powwow" was also the name of a gathering at which the medicine man presided. Such a function was usually a get-together for a tribe or tribal group where problems of the group could be discussed. Here the pipe might be passed around and smoked, and there could be dancing, singing and prayers. Perhaps the powwow himself would offer aid and counsel.

Games

The Indians of New England worked hard; the women with planting, hoeing, weaving and household tasks; the men, on the long treks through the forest in search of game. But there was still time for play, and they had many games. These included *baggataway* or lacrosse, the Indian invention later adopted by the Canadians as their national game. It was basically the same game as the one played today in schools and colleges, but much rougher and with few rigid rules. Sometimes there would be as many as one or two hundred men on a side, and it has even been described as a relatively mild form of tribal warfare. But it was still a game.

There were also contests with the bow and arrow, various kinds of stick games, and the snow snake game. The latter required a long, straight trough on the snow or ice, usually made by dragging a log through the snow. Each player then tried to throw his "snake," a stave or pole polished to smoothness and with its forward end carved to resemble a snake's head, so that it would go as far as possible along the trough. With a snake which was well iced by a dip in freezing water, it is said that some players could achieve a distance of a mile.

In addition there were dice games and guessing games, for the Indians loved to gamble.

Some of these games (obviously) served to sharpen the skill of the Indian in the hunt and in warfare, but they were played for pleasure, and sometimes by the women too.

War

By nature or necessity, the New England Algonkian was not always a peaceful man. To him war itself was a kind of game, as well as a test of skill and courage that every brave must undergo. He delighted in creeping through the forest in the night to come upon the village of a rival tribe before daylight, attacking to the sound of shouts and war cries, killing or taking captives, or even merely touching his enemy, and scurrying off into the dawn before they could recover from their surprise. It mattered not that the rival tribe would sooner or later retaliate in the same fashion. That was something to be dealt with when it happened.

Scalping, incidentally, was little practiced among the New England Indians. Some authorities say it was not practiced at all until the coming of the white man. Then French and English, vying with each other for territory and power, began to offer the Indians sizeable sums, at first for the heads, but eventually for the more easily portable scalps, of their white and Indian enemies.

Nor was torture of captives, in those early days, as common as is generally believed. It does appear to have taken place at times, particularly when the captive was an especially hated enemy. To watch such a man endure torture, even laugh at it, was to the Indian a spectacle worth seeing. But this could hardly place him in savagery far from the customs of his white European contemporaries, who were still burning prisoners alive at the stake, pressing them to death between stones, or throwing them into rat-infested dungeons; who not long before had been subjecting them to the thumbscrew and the rack and—for some time thereafter—would be witnessing the hanging of criminals with apparent pleasure.

It has also been said that the Algonkian practiced cannibalism, but this does not seem to have been a general custom. It was more common among the Mohawks to the west, at least until the 1500s, when their great chief Hiawatha is said to have stopped the practice. The Mohawks' name in Algonkian meant "eaters of men," although they called themselves *"Kaniegehaga—*people of the place of the flint."

The Mohawks were members of the Iroquois or Five Nations Confederation, and even if the Algonkian had not been warlike by nature, he would have been forced to war for survival against this group. To the north in Canada, the Algonkians had sometimes proved more than a match for the Iroquois nations, but in New England, they could never quite match the tightly knit organization of the Five Nations. Perhaps, too, they could seldom match in fierceness the fighting Mohawk in battle. Nothing to them was more terrifying than the cry of the Mohawk out of the night: *"Hadree! Hadree! Succomee! Succomee!"* "(We come! We

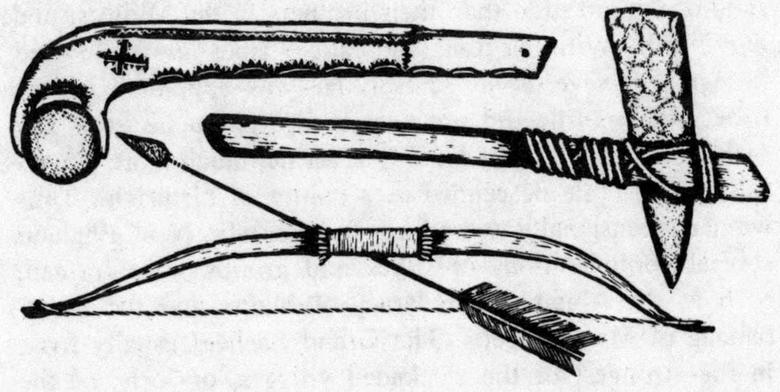

come! To suck your blood!") Sometimes it even drove the Algonkians to headlong, panic-stricken flight without battle.

The weapons of the New England Indian were simple by European standards of the time, making it difficult for him to compete against the sword and the musket. Still, properly handled and under the Indians' chosen conditions, they could be deadly. There was the bow and arrow, limited in range but effective within that range, also the stone knife, and sometimes the spear. The *atlate*, or throwing stick, had once been commonly used with the spear, particularly in hunting, for it gave greater range and accuracy, but it seems eventually to have been abandoned, after the invention of the bow.

The stone hatchet, or tomahawk, has already been described. More commonly used in war, at least until the coming of the steel hatchet, was the war club also called a tomahawk. This consisted of a wooden knob with a wooden handle two feet or more long. Sometimes the knob was set into the handle, and sometimes it was a knot of the tree from which the whole club was made. A piece of stone or bone could also be set into the knob for greater effectiveness, and the handle was often beautifully decorated.

The New England Indian often carried a wooden shield into battle, and even wore "rod" armor made of sticks of wood.

Political Structure

Perhaps it was the constant threat from the west which pushed the Algonkian tribes of New England to a higher state of organization than their brothers in the Midwest and Far North. With most of the latter tribes the chief had little power save as an advisor. He was appointed by the tribe, and his title did not necessarily fall to his son. The sachems of New England were, as a rule, much more powerful, and the title descended as a matter of birthright. Thus women occasionally served as sachems. In New England several confederations of tribes and groups were formed, such as the Abnaki Confederacy of Maine and the Wampanoag of Massachusetts. The Grand Sachem usually lived in the strongest of the stockaded villages, or forts, of the tribe, along with his sagamores. The sagamores, the "nobility" of the tribe, served as the sachem's advisors, and sometimes were leaders, in effect sachems, of smaller groups. In fact sometimes the two titles appear to be used interchangeably.

These confederations, where they existed, did strengthen the New England Algonkians, although they were not always enough in the face of the mighty Mohawk. Some of the tribes even paid tribute to the latter as protection.

The Indian's idea of possession was not that of the white man, and this was especially true when it came to land. To an Indian the land was part of his mother, the earth, something to be respected and used only as a steward might use it. When he sold to the white man, he thought it was only for the white man's use. He did not consider that he had given up his own right to roam, hunt and fish upon it. This attitude foreshadowed eventual bitter conflict.

(One recent authority, Alden T. Vaughan, takes issue with this commonly accepted view. He argues, with some proof to back his argument, that the Indian was perfectly aware of what he was selling. In the case of the early land deals made by the Pilgrim fathers, this may be true. It did not hold true with some of the later sales. And in any case, the Indian of the early days saw only a few white men in his country. He could hardly have envisioned the time when these would have so increased in numbers as to crowd his people to the point where they must give up entirely their own way of life.)

And in spite of his warlike ways, the Algonkian had many fine qualities. He would deceive an enemy if he could, but word given to a friend was held to be sacred. He loved his family, treating his children with such love and kindness that a white man of the time would have considered it spoiling them. Even captive white children were often adopted into the tribe, and sometimes came to prefer this life to the white man's way of living.

Few white men understood the Indian, and not many tried to do so. When John Eliot attempted to bring Christianity to them, even translating the Bible into an Indian tongue, Cotton Mather scornfully wrote: "To think of raising these hideous creatures into our holy religion! . . . Could he see anything angelical to encourage his labors? All was diabolical among them."

Nor did the early missionaries have marked success with their labors. Some Indians went so far as to say that the white man did not himself practice the religion he was attempting to foist upon them. Most Indians considered their own religion perfectly good, and most of them did practice it. And it is true that, while their worship had in it much of what we now consider childish magic, that worship was genuine. No worship in any religion could excel the Indian's love of the woods, the meadows, the streams around him and the sky above, nor his true reverence for all living creatures.

It was also often said by the early white settlers that the Indian was a filthy savage, with no thought of any kind about cleanliness. There was probably some truth in the claim, but we must not forget that the Puritans themselves were opposed to bathing. They felt that the nudity necessary in taking a bath was sinful. One European queen boasted she had bathed but twice in her life. And it has been said on good authority that the later white pioneers never took off their underwear from autumn to spring, at which point they threw it away and plunged into the nearest stream. Conditions often dictate the amount of cleanliness possible, and a bark wigwam with a dirt floor and only a small fire burning in the center is hardly suitable for regular bathing.

It is quite possible that the "filthy" Algonquin, as the winter stretched on, often felt as did the Paiute of the West who sang;

> "Oh, long, long
> The snow has possessed the mountains . . .
> We are wearied of our huts
> And the smoky smell of our garments.
> We are sick with desire of the sun
> And the grass on the mountain."

THE INDIAN IN MASSACHUSETTS AND RHODE ISLAND

There is archaeological evidence, in the Bull Brook site north of Ipswich, that the Indians were in Massachusetts at least 9,000 years ago. In 1951 a bulldozer unearthed fluted spear points of flint at that spot and since that time about a hundred of them have been found there. Possibly the date of the first arrival will be pushed back further in time with other such discoveries, but it can hardly go beyond the time of withdrawal of the last part of the Laurentian glacier from the area, about 13,500 years ago.

These would have been people of the late Paleo-Indian Epoch and presumably proto-Algonkians, early types of that particular linguistic group which spread over so much of North America. We cannot know the names of the tribes, or if they even had names. Probably they were simply groups of nomadic hunters of big game, with no true tribal organization, going where they could find the best hunting, or in this case heading for the seashore in search of lobsters, clams and other shellfish. Certainly they must have traveled from as far as what is now New York State, for the flint from which the points were chiseled could not be found any nearer. Further there is not much known about them, save that having worked their way to the seashore, as a people they disappeared. Obviously they were wiped out, or absorbed by, the Algonkians who later appeared on the scene.

These later people had a higher degree of culture, settled down in villages, planted corn, and so in time ceased to be nomadic. Probably, as previously mentioned, they had some relationship to the Hopewell Indians and to the Delaware, or Lenni Lenape. Yet among the Wampanoag of Massachusetts and Rhode Island, the ceremonial smoking of the pipe, carried down through countless generations, does not indicate a migration from the west. The smoker first faces to the east, from which the sun appears, then to the south, "from whence our ancestors came." Perhaps these Indians came eastward to the sea, then, in later generations, northward and up the Hudson, and so into New England, but that is only a guess.

At any rate, they were already well settled in scores of villages, a number of tribes and confederations of tribes, by the time the white man first appeared upon the horizon from across the sea. Then history—that is, white man's history—began for the Indians of the area.

This could have been more than 900 years ago, if it is true, as often claimed, that the Norseman visited the coast at that time. But it seems more likely, on the basis of such evidence as we have, that Leif Ericson's discovery of "Vinland," and the subsequent battle with the "Skraelings," (Indians) took place farther north, in the present-day Nova Scotia. Probably Sebastian Cabot did sail along the coast in 1498 and set foot upon New England soil. From that time on fishing vessels by the hundreds came from Europe for the good catches along the Grand Banks, and often anchored in Nova Scotia harbors, and they were followed by exploratory voyages of captains seeking to find out what they could of this new land and the possibilities of trade for profit with the inhabitants.

The history of the Indian in this area up to the early 1500s consists of lean but expressive finds of archaeologists and the accounts of the Indian himself. These latter were, of course, verbal tales often generations old, which many historians consider too subject to possible embroidering and errors of memory to be dependable. Nevertheless, they had been passed down through the tribes with great care, often told yearly before the same audiences so that no errors could creep in. They may well have been more accurate than many of the extremely biased written accounts which white historians would be giving of the Indians for the next two hundred years and more.

At that time there were in the area six separate groups of Indians, most of these confederations of several tribes, with somewhere between seventy and a hundred villages, scattered from the Atlantic Coast to the Berkshire or Tagonic hills of Western Massachusetts. In the latter area were the Mahicans, probably fairly close relatives of the great Lenni Lenape. At one time the Mahicans seem to have ranged from the Hudson River as far east as the Connecticut River, but by the time the white men met with them their numbers had diminished to a few groups along the Housatonic, stretching from the Connecticut border or a bit south, well into Vermont.

With the Mahicans we are fortunate in having an excellent account of the kind of tribal history which was passed down through the centuries. This was a speech made by John W. Quinney *(Waun-nau-con)*, a member of the tribe, on July 4, 1854, and written down at the time:

> A great people came from the Northwest: crossed over the salt-waters, and after long and weary pilgrimages, (planting many colonies on their track) took possession, and built their fires upon the Atlantic coast, extending from the Delaware on the south, to the Penobscot on the north. They became, in process of time, divided into different tribes and interests; all, however, speaking one common dialect. This great confederacy, comprising Delawares, Munsees, Mohegans, Narragansets, Pequots, Penobscots, and many others (of whom a few are now scattered among the distant wilds of the West—others supporting a weak, tottering existence, while, by far, a larger remainder have passed that bourne to which their brethren are tending) held its Council once a year, to deliberate on the general welfare. . . .
>
> The tribe, to which your speaker belongs, and of which there were many bands, occupied and possessed the country from the seashore, at Manhattan, to Lake Champlain. Having found an ebb and flow of the tide, they said: 'This is *Muh-he-ka-neew*, like our waters, which are never still.' From this expression and by this name, they were afterwards known, until their removal to Stockbridge, in the year 1730. Housatonic River Indians, Mohegans, Manhattas, were all names of bands in different localities, but bound together, as one family, by blood, marriage and descent. . . .

According to Quinney, this knowledge had come down at least from a Grand Council convened by King Ben, last of their hereditary chiefs, about 1645, "for the purpose of conveying from the old to the young a knowledge of the past." These councils, for this reason, "had ever, at stated periods, been held. Here, for the space of two moons, the stores of memory were dispensed; corrections and comparisons made, and the results committed to faithful breasts, to be transmitted again to succeeding posterity."

Perhaps it is incorrect to speak of this as "tribal history." It seems to be rather a history of all the Algonkian peoples of New England, despite the fact that it would not pass the present-day test of history. It is worth noting that it does present a clear statement of the Indians' crossing of the Bering Strait, at present the most commonly accepted theory of his appearance in North America. Yet it was written down in 1854, at a time when few white anthropologists or historians would have accepted this theory. Many were then propounding the belief, backed up with some apparent evidence, that the Indian was a member of one of the ten lost tribes of Israel. Even as late as 1904, at least one historian dismissed the Bering Strait theory as nonsense.

The Mahicans tended to be a peaceful tribe, more so than their powerful neighbors to the east, the Pocumtucks. With their principal fort and village at Pocumtuck, now Deerfield, this latter confederacy of seven tribes and at least 5,000 tribesmen dominated the Connecticut Valley from Hartford to Brattleboro.

East of the Pocumtuck were the Nipmucks who were also called—depending upon the Englishman who heard the name—Nipmunks and Nipnets. *Nipmaug*, "fresh water fishing place," was its original form. There were an estimated 500 Nipmucks in 1600, with around thirty villages spread from what is now southern Worcester County down into northeastern Connecticut and northern Rhode Island. They were not a tightly knit tribe for from time to time one or more of these villages would be attached, no doubt for protection, to one of the more powerful tribes or confederacies in the area, such as the Massachuset, Wampanoag, Narraganset, or the Mohegan-Pequot of Connecticut.

Probably the most powerful of all tribes or confederacies in the Massachusetts-Rhode Island area, in the early 1500s, was the Massachuset, which covered a good part of the northeastern area of the state that would later adopt the tribal name. This confederacy had around 3,000 warriors and more than twenty villages. Next, if not equal in size was the Wampanoag confederation to the south of the Massachuset. Pokanokut was the name of the principal tribe, which had its headquarters at Sowams (Barrington) and later Montaup or Mount Hope Neck, near Bristol, Rhode Island. The name Wampanoag came, according to some sources from the fact that these Indians produced a great deal of wampum, a valuable item in trade with other tribes in the surrounding areas. This confederation included, among others, the Nauset and Saconnet Indians of Cape Cod and the Nemaskets of Middleborough. It is said that the group, in its best days, included as many as 6,000 warriors, and thirty villages.

Occupying nearly all of Rhode Island west of Narragansett Bay was the great and powerful Narraganset tribe, allied with and related to the Nehantics or Niantics of western Rhode Island and eastern Connecticut. The Narragansets were long-time enemies of the Wampanoag.

In addition, the Pennacook must be mentioned here. The bulk of this confederation lived in New Hampshire, but they had at least seven villages in northeastern Massachusetts, among them Agawam (Ipswich) and Naumkeag (Salem).

The several confederacies, which usually contained more than one tribe and over which a Grand Sachem (Massasoit) ruled, were quite possibly born out of necessity, for hostile tribes surrounded the area. The Mohegan-Pequot, never averse to war and conquest, held sway to the south in Connecticut and from the west in New York State the Mohawk, fierce fighters all and backed by the powerful Iroquois Confederation, came to raid and collect tribute.

Equally fierce and nearly as powerful were the Abnaki to the north. This confederation, based principally in Maine, often warred with the then powerful Massachuset. Early accounts speak of them as the Tarentyns or Tarratines, but this name seems also to have been applied at one time to the Penobscots, at another to the invading Micmacs from Canada.

For the most part, the Indians of the coast welcomed as friends the first white men who came ashore. In addition to useless but appealing gewgaws, the newcomers had many things of value to offer them in trade—needles and awls, metal cooking pots and hatchets, blankets and clothing more comfortable than deerhide. Perhaps most important of all, the white man had guns. When he could get them, the Indian found them beyond value in both hunting and warfare, and soon became more proficient in their use than the white man.

It is surprising, in view of what soon happened, that the friendship continued as long as it did.

Twenty-six years after Cabot sailed up the coast of New England, came Giovanni da Verrazano, an Italian explorer employed by Francis I of France. Verrazano sailed into New York Bay and found it a busy place even then. From there he went on to present-day Newport, Rhode Island, where he found "the most beautiful people and the most civilized in customs . . . they excel us in size; they are of bronze color." These, presumably, were Narraganset Indians. Obviously, they were friendly to the visiting white men.

Verrazano did not find the Indians in Maine as friendly. Possibly they had already had some contact of an unpleasant sort with white men, for by now ships were beginning to cross over from Europe in increasing numbers, first to fish offshore for the great schools of cod, and eventually to trade with natives for furs. By the time the next real voyage of discovery occurred, that of Bartholomew Gosnold in 1602, these trading and fishing vessels were arriving each year literally by the hundreds.

Gosnold sailed the coast from Maine to Narragansett Bay, gave Cape Cod its name, and returned to England to promote the establishment of colonies in the areas he had explored. In 1604 Samuel de Champlain of France explored and mapped the New England coast as far south as Cape Cod. He made friends with the Indians wherever he met them, for he wished to study their customs and take his knowledge back to Europe. He was more interested in exploration and trade than in colonization.

The picture began to change a bit the following year, when Captain George Weymouth appeared off the coast of Maine, on a voyage of exploration and trade. Weymouth had been sent over by Sir Ferdinando Gorges, captain of the Port of Plymouth in England, who had eventual colonization of the newly explored lands in mind. Apparently Weymouth lured five Indians aboard his ship and sailed off with them to England. Among them, according to some accounts, was Squanto, also known as Tisquantum, who would return to New England at a fortunate time for the Pilgrims. These Indians were kidnapped not to be sold into slavery, but to be exhibited as curiosities and also to be studied by Gorges, who wished to learn more about the new land to the westward and its inhabitants. Some of them were later allowed to return home.

The next man to arrive worth noting was Captain John Smith. He came in 1614, and in the course of mapping the coast of New England from Penobscot south, and bartering with the Indians for beaver and other furs, he landed at Nauset. He found the Nausets friendly at first, but a quarrel broke out between them and his men, apparently the fault of the Englishmen rather than the Indians. A pitched battle followed, in which several of the Nausets were killed. The rest, having used up all their arrows, retreated into the woods.

In spite of this, Smith was determined to do his trading. Somehow, whether due to the fact that he was no mean diplomat or because of the naturally friendly disposition of the Nausets, the latter came back before the day was over as if nothing untoward had happened. Smith got his bartering in at that time and acquired a few furs.

Apparently this incident left no lasting scars among the Indians, but unfortunately, when Smith sailed for England in one of his two ships, he left the second behind to complete its cargo of fish and furs, with orders to sell the fish in Spain. In the course of carrying out his instructions, the master of the ship, Captain Thomas Hunt, decoyed twenty-four Nausets on board and set sail for Spain where he sold them as slaves for twenty pounds a head.

Smith himself, when he learned of this, concluded that Hunt had acted in this reprehensible fashion not so much for the immediate profit as to further a long-range plan to keep the natives hostile, "thereby to keep this abounding country still in obscurity, that only he and some few merchants more might enjoy wholly the benefit of the trade." Hunt was dismissed from employment upon his return to England, but the damage had been done. The friends and relations of the captured Nausets would not forget.

Nor was this all by any means. Nearly a hundred years before, both Verrazano and Jacques Cartier had kidnapped Indians along the New England coast, usually trusting and friendly ones, and taken them to Europe never to return to their homes. Most of them died in captivity. Captain Edward Harlow continued the practice when mapping the coast in 1611, seizing six Indians, one of whom escaped. The other five eventually fell into the hands of Gorges, and some of them got home again. Among these latter was Epenow, a native of Capâwock (Martha's Vineyard) described in white men's terms as "cunning" and "artful," who "had been treacherously brought to England by one of the fishing ships" to be exhibited.

Sir Ferdinando Gorges who sent various expeditions to New England, determined eventually to colonize a large tract of land he had been granted by the King. These expeditions had returned with considerable knowledge of the land and the natives, but nothing else. No colonists had poured across the sea to settle in Gorges' feudal domain, and his associates lost interest. Gorges did not, and soon determined to try again, this time with a scheme which seemed to promise financial returns. This is where Epenow came in, and his story can best be told in the words of W. C. Armstrong, in his *The Life and Adventures of Captain John Smith:*

> This savage came to Gorges with Captain Henry Harley, an unfortunate adventurer in the first expedition, who anticipated great results from what he had been told by him respecting his native country. The fellow, it seems, had invented a plausible story relative to a mine of gold in his native island, in the hope that some adventurer would be induced to convey him home, to point out the treasure; nor was he disappointed. Funds were soon raised, and Harley sailed in June, 1614, taking with him Epenow and two other Indians, named Assacumet and Wanapé.
>
> On the arrival of the ship at the harbor where Epenow was to fulfil his promise, many of his kinsmen and other natives came on board, with whom he held a conference, and contrived his escape. When leaving, they promised to return the next day with furs for traffic. Epenow had pretended that if it were known that he had betrayed the secrets of his country, his life would be in danger, but the company were careful to watch him; and to prevent his escape, had

> dressed him in long clothes, which could easily be laid hold of, if there should be occasion.
>
> His friends appeared the next morning in twenty canoes; and, lying at a distance, the captain called on them to come on board, which they declining, Epenow was ordered to renew the invitation. He, mounting the forecastle, hailed them as he was directed, and at the same instant, though one held him by the coat, yet being strong and heavy, he jumped into the water. His countrymen then advanced to receive him, and sent a shower of arrows into the ship, which so disconcerted the crew, that the prisoner completely effected his escape.

Harley gave up his high hopes of fortune and sailed back to England, and Gorges was some pounds poorer. But Epenow got back to his home and family.

He was luckier than most, or perhaps wiser than most. One ship's captain, having gotten enough Indians aboard his ship to provide him with all the furs he could carry home, simply turned his men loose with their muskets and slaughtered the lot of them.

How many more white captains—traders, fishermen and adventurers—killed Indians without cause or seized them and took them off to Europe to be sold as slaves is not known. The above includes only the most notable of the recorded cases. There may be some indication in the fact that by 1620 the market for Indian slaves in Spain had ceased to exist. Probably that market was glutted, and at any rate the Spaniards had found that the New England Indians did not take kindly to enslavement, and so were "treacherous" and did not make satisfactory slaves.

Certainly they did not take kindly to the other outrages they suffered at the hands of the white men, such as cheating by the traders, and this may have contributed in some part to the failure of the first settlement attempted by the English in New England. In 1607 the Plymouth Company sent out 120 colonists under George Popham and Raleigh Gilbert, who settled at the mouth of the Kennebec. But their supplies ran low, more than half of them went home, and in the following year the colony was abandoned. The natives had offered them neither aid nor friendship.

Thus was the stage set for the arrival of the Pilgrims.

THE SAINTS COME SAILING IN

On November 21, 1620 the ship *Mayflower* dropped anchor in Cape Cod Bay, two months and five days after leaving the harbor at Plymouth, England. Aboard the little vessel (180 tons and about 106 feet long) was a motley assortment of 102 passengers, "Saints" and "Strangers." The Saints (or Saincts) as they called themselves, were Separatists who had broken away from the Church of England and gone to live in Holland. They were welcomed there, but soon found themselves lonely in a strange land. Now they saw a chance to better themselves by going to America. There they could live as they wished and probably gain some profit from the venture as well. Having little in goods or money of their own, they had been financed for the voyage by the English company of "Merchant Adventurers." The merchant adventurers of course, expected to turn a considerable profit through the furs, gold and whatever riches America had to offer, which these Pilgrims would send to them, once they had gotten them from the Indians.

The Strangers were men not of their faith, belonging mainly to the Church of England, and had joined them before they sailed out of Plymouth harbor.

Four days after anchoring, sixteen men, armed with "musket, sword, and corslet," went ashore under the command of their hired soldier, Captain Myles Standish. They were not long on land before they spotted five or six Indians and a dog. The Indians fled into the woods at the sight of the Englishmen, calling their dog to follow them. These were Nauset Indians, who had had an unfortunate experience with Captain Hunt only a few years before.

Failing in their attempt to track down the Nausets, the party lit a fire, set out sentinels, and camped for the night. In the morning they set out again on the trail of the Nausets, following it through the woods across hills and valleys, but never could they spot an Indian again, or any sign of habitation. But they did find "certain heaps of sand, one whereof was covered with old mats, and a wooden thing like a mortar . . . on the top . . . and an earthen pot laid in a little hole in the ground." They dug down and found a bow and rotten arrows, but assuming by now that this was a grave, they put it back together as it had been and went on, "because we thought it would be odious unto them to ransack their sepulchres."

No harm done there, apparently, but next they came upon a store of Indian corn buried in the ground, and an iron kettle, probably a ship's kettle, alongside. They put all the corn they could carry into the kettle and made off with it, intending, they said, when they later met up with the people, "to satisfy them for their corn." Unfortunately, the Indians could hardly be aware of this good intent.

They also made off with the Indian-made rope from a snare for catching deer. These things accomplished, along with some further exploration of the land, they returned to the ship.

A few days later, after they had repaired their shallop— a large, open boat fitted with both oars and a sail— a larger party, this time twenty-four armed men, went down the bay for further exploration. They went ashore where they had previously found the corn, (at Cornhill, in what is now Truro) and this time they found a large store of it, all of ten bushels, "which will serve us sufficiently for seed," says the writer of *Mourt's Relation.* "And sure it was God's good providence that we found this corn, for else we know not how we should have done, for we knew not how we should find or meet with any Indians, except it be to do us mischief." They also found more graves, and no longer seemed to have any compunctions that it might "be odious unto them to ransack their sepulchres," for they "brought sundry of the prettiest things away" from a child's grave and covered the corpse up again. They also found two Indian dwellings from which the occupants had apparently temporarily absented themselves and "some of the best things we took away with us." It was the intention of the Pilgrims, the narrator says, to have brought back beads and other items to leave in the wigwams as payment for what they had taken, but somehow they did not find the time to do so.

Under the circumstances, it is hardly surprising that the next time these industrious explorers came ashore they ran into some opposition. They first spotted a group of Indians flensing a "grampus" (probably in this case a blackfish) that had been washed ashore, but the Indians fled at the sight of them, taking most of the meat they had cut. The Pilgrims tried to follow their trail, but soon lost it in the woods. Late in the day their shallop came in sight and stood off, waiting. They camped near the shore that night, and in the morning prepared to embark as soon as they had breakfasted, having already carried their heavy armor down to the shore, including most of their muskets.

This was the moment the Indians awaited. With a "great and strange cry," they appeared from the woods and loosed a barrage of arrows.

The Pilgrims "ran out with all speed" to get their muskets, but one at least had not let his out of reach. This was Captain Myles Standish, a little man but obviously a tough soldier. Furthermore, he possessed a snaphance, a kind of flintlock musket more quickly ready to fire than the matchlocks which most of the others carried. He fired at the Indians at once, "and after him another." Soon the rest had recovered their muskets and were ready to fire with time to take aim. One even took a burning log from the campfire and carried it out to the shallop so that the men out there could make use of their matchlocks, "which was thought did not a little discourage our enemies."

Nevertheless the Indians came on, crying a "dreadful" cry which sounded to the Englishmen like *"Woach woach ha ha hach woach."* One, "a lusty man and no whit less valiant, who was thought to be their captain, stood behind a tree within half a musket shot of us, and there let his arrows fly at us." His arrows did not strike their targets, and he himself "stood three shots of a musket," but at the fourth "he gave an extraordinary cry and away they went all."

Actually he had apparently been hit only by a flying splinter of wood from the tree, and there were no casualties on the English side. The Indians, having used up all their arrows, retired from the scene. "Thus" says the author of *Mourt's Relation,* "it pleased God to vanquish our enemies and give us deliverance." The Pilgrims, failing in their attempt to follow the Indians, also soon retired from the scene in their shallop. They named that place The First Encounter, and a beach in Eastham, thought to be the same one, is so called to this day.

Had something changed the Nausets who, only fifteen years before, Champlain had first described as "not only numerous and industrious, but very friendly"?

At any rate, the Pilgrims had begun to have their doubts about settling on Cape Cod, despite its rich soil and excellent fishing. Already a party had gone across to the far side of the bay to investigate the possibilities surrounding a harbor mapped by Champlain and named Port du Cap. St. Louis, and later noted by Captain John Smith during his mapping of the coast. He had asked the then Prince Charles to give English names to various points on the map of this "barbarian" land, and this one got the name of "Plimouth."

Here they found high ground, good soil and even corn ground already cleared by the former Indian inhabitants, who had been wiped out by the "Plague." And here they decided to settle. They landed on December 21, though it is by no means certain they landed on Plymouth Rock.

The conquest of "Northern Virginia," or New England as it is now called, had begun.

It must not be supposed that before the English began to settle in New England, all was peaceful and serene among the Indians. As has already been mentioned, Wampanoag and Narraganset clashed from time to time. The Mahicans were pushed eastward by the pugnacious Mohawks of the Iroquois Confederation, although in time this appears to have been settled by a treaty. But as late as the 1600s, the Mohawks and the Pocumtucks, one-time allies, engaged in a fierce war which all but wiped out the latter.

Undoubtedly the greatest threat to the Massachusetts tribes, and particularly to the Massachuset Confederation, was the Abnaki. This latter confederation consisted principally of the Abnaki, the Malecites, the Passamaquoddys, and the Penobscots, while the Pennacooks of New Hampshire and northeastern Massachusetts were at times at least loosely allied to them. It has been said that in the early

1600s there were as many as 25,000 Indians in the confederation, but such early figures tend to be greatly exaggerated. At any rate, they probably made up the most powerful confederation in New England, were fierce and unrelenting fighters, and were said sometimes to eat their victims. They frequently raided the tribes to the south, particularly those along the coast.

But in the early 1600s the Massachuset Confederation was also strong, with more than 20 villages and perhaps 3,000 warriors—strong enough, in the opinion of their Grand Sachem Nanepashemet (the New Moon) to retaliate against the Abnaki. His warriors swept up the coast to Maine, raided several villages, wreaked general havoc, and carried off many captives. When the Abnaki offered to ransom the captives, Nanepashemet arrogantly refused.

Then, at some time between 1615 and 1619 (the dates given vary) what was known as the Great Plague struck. It was not bubonic plague and it was not smallpox; modern authorities believe it may have been a relatively mild disease such as measles. Visiting Europeans were immune to it, but Indians were not, and some believed that the white man's god had thus struck them down as punishment. From this it is reasonable to suspect that it indeed came to them from white sailors and traders.

It did not strike as far north as Maine, nor did it touch the Narraganset in Rhode Island. The Wampanoag felt it, and it may even have gone as far as the Mahican in Western Massachusetts—but most of all, it struck down the people of Nanepashemet. Thousands died, until there were not enough left to bury the dead and they were stacked one upon another like cordwood.

Now the tribes of the Massachuset Confederation had lost their strength; now the Abnaki could sail down in their war canoes and gain their revenge upon Nanepashemet.

Gone was the arrogance of the Grand Sachem. Trembling in his terror, he fled from his village. Having gathered his most faithful followers about him, a few miles inland he built a sort of tree-house fortress—or to be more exact, a house on stilts—and waited for the certain coming of the Abnaki. But perhaps the "fortress" can best be described in the words of one of the first white men to look upon it, as told in *Mourt's Relation:*

> Having gone three miles we came to a place where corn had been newly gathered, a house pulled down, and the people gone. A mile from hence, Nanepashemet, their king, in his life-time had lived. His house was not like others, but a scaffold was largely built, with poles and planks some six feet from ground, and the house upon that, being situated on the top of a hill.
>
> Not far from hence, in a bottom, we came to a fort built by their deceased king, the manner thus: there were poles some thirty or forty feet long, stuck in the ground as thick as they could be set one by another, and with these they enclosed a ring some forty or fifty feet over. A trench breast high was digged on each side; one way there was to go into it with a bridge; in the midst of this palisade stood the frame of a house wherein, being dead, he lay buried.
>
> About a mile from hence, we came to such another, but seated on top of a hill; here Nanepashemet was killed, none dwelling in it since the time of his death. . . .

For the Abnaki had not been long in coming, and the fortresses of Nanepashemet availed him little. They killed him and slaughtered many of his tribe as well. Now, in 1621, his widow, known as Squaw Sachem, ruled over what was left of the Massachuset Confederation. This once great and powerful group had been reduced to a remnant of its former self.

BITTER WINTER AND BRIGHT SPRING

As anyone who has ever lived in New England can testify, late December is a poor time to land on the coast without shelter. No doubt these Pilgrims were hardy souls, convinced that God was on their side and had brought them here to convert the heathen and do good in other ways. "Their land [the Indians] is empty," they reasoned, and besides it [America] "is proper to the King of England." And they set to work at once to build themselves rude, thatched-roof huts. Nevertheless, more than half of them died that first winter of pneumonia and other diseases, and by the time the winter ended they were running short of food and other necessary supplies.

Throughout the first month ashore there was little sign of their Indian neighbors, and the few they did catch sight of kept their distance. Once, they helped themselves to some English tools left lying about. Late in February, "two savages presented themselves upon the top of a hill, over against our plantation . . . and made signs unto us to come unto them; we likewise made signs unto them to come to us, whereupon we armed ourselves, and stood ready, and sent . . . Captain Standish and Stephen Hopkins . . . towards them. Only one of them [the Englishmen] had a musket, which they laid down on the ground in their sight, in sign of peace, and to parley with them, but the savages would not tarry their coming. A noise of a great many more was heard behind the hill, but no more came in sight. This caused us to plant our ordnances in places most convenient. . . ." [Mourt's Relation]

Perhaps these "savages" had been warned by their neighbors on the Cape.

Then, about a month later, "there presented himself a savage, which caused an alarm. He very boldly came all alone and along the houses straight to the rendezvous [for military organization] where we intercepted him, not suffering him to go in, as undoubtedly he would, out of his boldness. He saluted us in English, and bade us welcome. . . . He was a man free in speech . . . and of a seemingly carriage . . . a tall straight man. . . ." [Mourt's Relation]

This was Samoset, a sachem or sagamore from Monhegan Island, off southeastern Maine, who had learned broken English from the Englishmen who came there to fish. He had been visiting in these parts for some months, and thus could and did tell the Pilgrims freely of the number of Indians in the area, their strength and their sagamores or sachems. While not at first inclined to be hospitable to him, they did now, "the wind beginning to rise a little," put a coat about his shoulders, since he was clad only in his leather loincloth. Eventually they gave him food and drink.

The place where the Pilgrims had settled, he told them, was called Patuxet, and four years before all the inhabitants had died of the plague, "so as there is none to hinder our possession, or to lay claim unto it." This the Pilgrims were quick to interpret as an act of God designed to clear the way for them, proving that their venture had devine approval.

At the end of an afternoon of talk, the Englishmen hoped their uninvited guest would go, but he did not. Finally they lodged him in Stephen Hopkins' house, and watched him.

Samoset told them the Nausets were "much incensed and provoked against the English . . . by reason of one Hunt, a master of a ship, who deceived the people, and got them under color of trucking [trading] with them, twenty out of this very place where we inhabit, and seven men from the Nausets, and carried them away, and sold them for slaves like a wretched man . . . that cares not what mischief he doth for profit." In fact, the Nausets had killed three Englishmen of Captain Thomas Dermer's ship only eight months before.

Samoset left the following morning to return to Sowams, the Pokanokut village of Massasoit, headquarters of the Wampanoag Confederation of which Massasoit was Grand Sachem. He promised to return within a night or two, bringing with him some of Massasoit's men and such beaver skins as they had to offer in trade. This last was very important to the Pilgrims, since beaver skins were a principal item by which they hoped to repay their debt to the merchant adventurers in England who had financed this venture.

Two days later Samoset returned, bringing with him "five other tall proper men," who also brought a few skins for trade, and within the next week Samoset came again. This time he was accompanied by one Squanto, who would play a considerable part in the early history of the Pilgrim colony. He was the only remaining native of Patuxet or Plymouth, and appeared to have learned more English than had Samoset. The reason for this, as the Pilgrims tell it in *Mourt's Relation,* and as he reputedly told it to them, was that he "was one of the twenty captives that by Hunt were carried away, and had been in England, and dwelt in Cornhill with Master John Slanie, a merchant. . . ." If this were the whole story, then he would have had to escape from his Spanish master, and speaking no English or other European language at the time, traveled halfway across Europe as a fugitive slave and still made his way by some odd chance to England. This truly would be material for one of the great sagas of all time. But William Brandon, in *The American Heritage Book of Indians,* advances with some documentation the theory that there were two Squantos—one whose full name was Tasquantum and the other's Tisquantum. One he believes was captured by Hunt and taken to Spain, and perhaps never heard of again; the other, the Squanto the Pilgrims met, had been taken by Captain George Weymouth to England, turned over to Master Slanie and eventually to Sir Ferdinando Gorges, and in time allowed to return home, where he found himself the sole survivor of his village. This seems the more plausible if less dramatic explanation than the previously accepted one.

But there is also a third explanation, one offered by George F. Willison in his *Saints and Strangers* and by other authorities. These writers believe that there was but one Squanto and that he was twice captured—first by Weymouth and then by Hunt. It seems at first thought incredible that he would have fallen into the trap the second time, but we must remember that the first time he was fairly well treated and eventually allowed to return home, and thus may have come to trust Englishmen. At least it would explain how he had gained enough knowledge of the language and of European ways to escape from the Spaniards "by the assistance of certain kindly-disposed monks" [Brownell] and make his way to England. On balance, it seems the most likely answer to the puzzle, and thus demolishes the makings of a saga.

However, on this particular day when Squanto first appeared in the company of Samoset, it was principally to inform the Englishmen that Ousamequin or Massasoit, Grand Sachem of the Wampanoag Confederation, (Massasoit was in fact his title, not his name) was come over from his base at Sowams to parley with them. With him came his brother Quadequina and sixty warriors. Shortly thereafter the Indians appeared at the top of a nearby hill, gifts were sent by the Pilgrims to Massasoit and his brother, and Edward Winslow went out as a messenger to parley with them.

"Our messenger made a speech unto him, that King James saluted him with words of love and peace, and did accept him as his friend and ally, and that our governor desired to see him and to truck with him, and to confirm a peace with him, as his next neighbor. He liked well of the speech, and heard it attentively. . . ." [Bradford]

After some further preliminaries, Massasoit, "a very lusty man, in his best years, grave of countenance, and spare of speech," and some of his men came down to the village, where the governor awaited them, and they treated of peace, which was:

> 1. That neither he nor any of his would injure or do hurt to any of our people.
> 2. And if any of his did hurt to any of ours, he should send the offender, that we might punish him.
> 3. That if any of our tools were taken away when our people were at work, he should cause them to be restored, and if ours did any harm to any of his, we would do the like to them.
> 4. If any did unjustly war against him, we would aid him; if any did war against us, he should aid us.
> 5. He should send to his neighbor confederates, to certify them of this, that they might not wrong us, but might be likewise comprised in the conditions of peace.
> 6. That when their men came to us, they should leave their bows and arrows behind them, as we should do our pieces when we came to them.
>
> Lastly, that doing thus, King James would esteem of him as his friend and ally.
>
> All of which the king seemed to like well, and it was applauded of his followers. . . . [Bradford]

This treaty or security pact was kept by Massasoit as long as he lived, and in fact was not broken until 1675, 13 years after his death. Nevertheless, it contained elements that would prove of far greater advantage to the English than to the Indians, as will appear later, and so it held the seed of future dissension. Most of all, it put the foot of the English firmly inside the door, and that foot was never dislodged. It may at the time have been "applauded of his followers," but there were Indians not much later who would call Massasoit a traitor to his race for making the agreement. Why then, did he do so, when if he wished he could have wiped out the tiny colony?

The most commonly accepted explanation is that he looked to the English and their muskets, few as they were, for strength. His people had been badly hit by the plague, not as badly as the Massachuset, but enough to weaken them and perhaps weaken the loose bonds of the confederation as well. His nearest neighbors to the south and west, the Narraganset tribe and its allies, were also his enemies. The plague had not touched them, and Massasoit felt that at any time they might attack the Wampanoag group and destroy it.

Most of all, Massasoit was basically a man of peace. He governed his people not with harshness but with kindness and compassion, and with respect and affection that they gave to him in return. Had he listened to Corbitant, a sagamore or lesser sachem and one of his wise councillors, there would have been war before the year was out. Corbitant seemed to have foreseen the future, for he wanted to wipe out the little English colony while it was still weak. Had his advice prevailed, the history of America might have been quite different, but Massasoit wanted none of this. He saw in the agreement a promise of peace, and as long as he lived he had it, although as time went on he seemed to have entertained some doubts and disappointments.

What this peace cost his people is something else again.

A LOST BOY

For a little while, the agreement worked largely to the advantage of both Indians and whites. Other tribes came in to join the confederation over which Massasoit ruled, in part because of his new allies. At the same time the Englishmen learned much that was necessary for anyone living in this country to know, such as the proper means to plant their Indian corn, with a fish for fertilizer in each hill. They were also able now to travel freely about the nearby countryside, knowing that they were protected by Massasoit, and so finding friendly people wherever they went, as well as people who provided them with guidance and food. On one such journey Stephen Hopkins and Edward Winslow went as far as Pokanokut, the village of Massasoit. There Massasoit entertained them in his fashion, and they smoked tobacco with him and talked of many things. He spoke of the Frenchmen who often sailed up the bay, "bidding us not to suffer them to come to Narraganset, for it was King James his country, and he also was King James his man." In turn he asked all his people to bring their skins to the English at Plymouth for trade, which they agreed to do.

On another occassion, young John Billington wandered far from Plymouth and became lost in the woods, where he was picked up, or perhaps kidnapped, by the Cape Indians. Since these Indians had not yet forgotten the stolen corn, the robbed graves, and their battle with the English the preceding November, they surely held no love for the white-skinned newcomers, and it is probable that eventually they would have killed the boy. Fortunately for young John, the Pilgrims asked Massasoit to intercede. As the Cape Indians were his allies, he was able to do so.

This having been accomplished, on a bright June day in 1621, ten men set out in the shallop for the Cape. These ten included Squanto, their interpreter, and Tokamahamon,

a special friend. They anchored that night at Cummaquid (Barnstable). There they discovered that the boy was at Nauset (Eastham), but were invited by the men of Cummaquid to come ashore and eat with them. They agreed, but not until they were allowed to keep four of the Indians as hostage in their boat, with four white men to keep watch over them.

There they met the Cummaquid sachem, Iyanough, "a man not exceeding twenty-six years of age, but very personable, gentle, courteous, and fair conditioned, indeed not like a savage, save for his attire. His entertainment was answerable to his parts, and his cheer plentiful and various." (The name Hyannis is a variant spelling of Iyanough.)

One thing, however, was "very grievous" to them at this place.

> There was an old woman, whom we judged to be no less than a hundred years old, which came to see us because she never saw English, yet could not behold us without breaking forth into great passion, weeping and crying excessively. We demanding the reason of it, they told us she had three sons who, when Master Hunt was in these parts, went aboard his ship to trade with him, and he carried them captives into Spain (for Squanto at that time was carried away also) by which means she was deprived of the comfort of her children in her old age. We told them we were sorry that any Englishmen should give them that offense, that Hunt was a bad man, and that all the English that heard of it condemned him for the same; but for us, we would not offer them any such injury though it would gain us all the skins in the country. So we gave her some small trifles, which somewhat appeased her. [Mourt's Relation]

Eventually they sailed on for Eastham accompanied by Iyanough and two of his men. There these three went ashore, along with Squanto, who bore a message to Aspinet, the sachem of Nauset, advising him they had come for the Billington boy. Here the Nausets crowded about them "very thick" while the shallop was still afloat, but the Pilgrims "stood therein upon our guard," aware that these were the same Indians with whom they had fought the winter before. Finally they let two of them into the shallop, one being from Manomyik (Chatham) whose corn they had taken at that time. "We promised him restitution, and desired him either to come to Patuxet for satisfaction, or else we would bring them so much corn again. He promised to come. . . ." [Mourt's Relation]

Whether the Pilgrims ever did pay for the purloined corn is uncertain. They had previously asked Massasoit to take care of the matter for them, but apparently he had not done so, nor is there any record that the man from Chatham ever came to collect. Probably restitution never was made, and perhaps the Indians no longer felt it very important, now that summer was come and they had a new crop growing in the fields. But the robbing of the graves could not be so easily forgotten, as the English would find in a later instance.

Eventually Aspinet came with a great train and brought the Billington boy, "behung with beads, and made peace with us, we bestowing a knife on him. . . ."

From Aspinet, however, they learned startling news that sent them hurrying home. Massasoit had been captured by the Narragansets! The greatest protection of the weak little colony from hostile Indians was gone.

Once back in Plymouth, they found the problems even more complex. Corbitant, whom the Pilgrims feared as being too conversant with the Narragansets, was now at Nemasket (Middleborough) where he "sought to draw the hearts of Massasoit's subjects from him." He spoke disparagingly of the English, denouncing the peace between them and the Nauset and Cummaquid Indians, and of Squanto, who had in his opinion brought it about. He also denounced Tokamahamon and Hobbomok, two Indians friendly to the Pilgrims. Hobbomok, according to William Bradford "a proper lustie man, and a man of accounte for his vallour and parts amongst the Indians," had in fact come to Plymouth to live in the Pilgrim village.

Upon word of the capture of Massasoit and of Corbitant's doings, Tokamahamon had gone directly to the sagamore, apparently to reason with him. Squanto and Hobbomok, not quite so willing to walk into the lion's mouth, went to Nemasket to try to get some word on Massasoit. While staying there they were informed upon to Corbitant. Immediately he set a guard upon the house where they were staying, and came in himself to take Squanto. Holding a knife at his breast, he is reputed to have said that if Squanto were dead, "the English had lost their tongue."

At this point Hobbomok, "being a strong and stout man, broke from them and came to New Plymouth, full of fear and sorrow for Squanto, whom he thought to be slain."

The next morning, before daylight, the Pilgrims gathered together ten armed men, who set out for Nemasket with Hobbomok for their guide. They intended to avenge the death of Squanto, presumably by killing Corbitant, and also to "retain" Nepeof, another sachem of the Wampanoag, till they could learn what had happened to Massasoit. They spent the night three or four miles from Nemasket, and marched on in the morning to surround the house of Corbitant, while some went inside and demanded to know if the sagamore were there.

In the words of *Mourt's Relation,* "fear had bereft the savages of speech. We charged them not to stir, for if Corbitant were not there, we would not meddle with them; if he were, we came principally for him, to be avenged on him for the supposed death of Squanto, and other matters; but, however, we would not at all hurt their women or children. Notwithstanding, some of them pressed out at a private door and escaped, but with some wounds."

Finally the Indians regained their courage and speech enough to explain that Corbitant had gone elsewhere with all his train, and that Squanto was still alive. They offered the Pilgrims tobacco and food. Some of the boys in the house, seeing that the Englishmen were not hurting women, cried out *"Neen squaes,"* (I am a woman). Then Hobbomok climbed to the roof of the house where Squanto and Tokamahamon were held and called down to them. They came out, accompanied by some of the Nemaskets who were guarding them.

> On the next morning we marched into the midst of the town, and went to the house of Squanto to breakfast. Thither came all whose

hearts were upright towards us, but all Corbitant's faction were fled away. There in the midst of them we manifested again our intendment, assuring them, that although Corbitant had now escaped us, yet there was no place should secure him and his from us if he continued his threatening us and provoking others against us, who had kindly entertained him, and never intended evil towards him till he now so justly deserved it. Moreover, if Massasoit did not return in safety from Narraganset, or if hereafter he should make any insurrection against him, or offer violence to Squanto, Hobbomok, or any of Massasoit's subjects, we would revenge it upon him to the overthrow of him and his. As for those were wounded, we were sorry for it, though themselves procured it in not staying in the house at our command; yet if they would return home with us, our surgeon should heal them.

At this offer, one man and a woman that were wounded went home with us, Squanto and many other known friends accompanying us, and offering all help that might be by carriage of anything we had to ease us. So that, by God's good providence, we safely returned home the morrow night after we set forth.

These bold threats seem to have been effective, for a short time later Massasoit returned home unharmed. But Corbitant, convinced as he apparently was that the presence of these English colonists meant the eventual destruction of his people, had not been entirely subdued.

A DUBIOUS FRIEND

Flushed with their success thus far in dominating, or at least daunting, the Indians around them, in September of 1621 a party of ten Pilgrims, along with Squanto and two other Indians as interpreters, set out for a further voyage in their shallop. As told in *Mourt's Relation,* "It seemed good to the company in general, that though the Massachusets had often threatened us (as we were informed), yet we should go amongst them, partly to see the country, partly to make peace with them, and partly to procure their truck."

Thus they sailed up to Massachusetts Bay, went ashore and "marched in arms up in the country." They came to the village where Nanepashemet had lived before his death, as described earlier. They were unable to meet with his widow, the Squaw Sachem, but they did locate several of her subjects. Fearful at first, these people finally came to believe that the white men meant no harm. Eventually they engaged in a certain amount of trading, from which the English secured a few skins.

These friendly interchanges, easily earned, did not prove of lasting value, and a greater threat came not long after. Late that year the Narragansets sent a messenger to Plymouth with a bundle of arrows tied about with a great snakeskin—as Bradford puts it, "a threatening and a challenge."

Just a short time before this, the *Fortune* had sailed into Plymouth Harbor, bringing from England and Holland 35 more colonists, most of them "lusty yonge men." Now the little colony could afford to throw its weight around, with something to back it up. Governor Bradford sent the snakeskin back filled with bullets, along with a message to the Narragansets, saying "that if they had rather have warre then peace, they might begine when they would. [The Pilgrims] had done them no wrong, nor did they fear them, or should they find them unprovided."

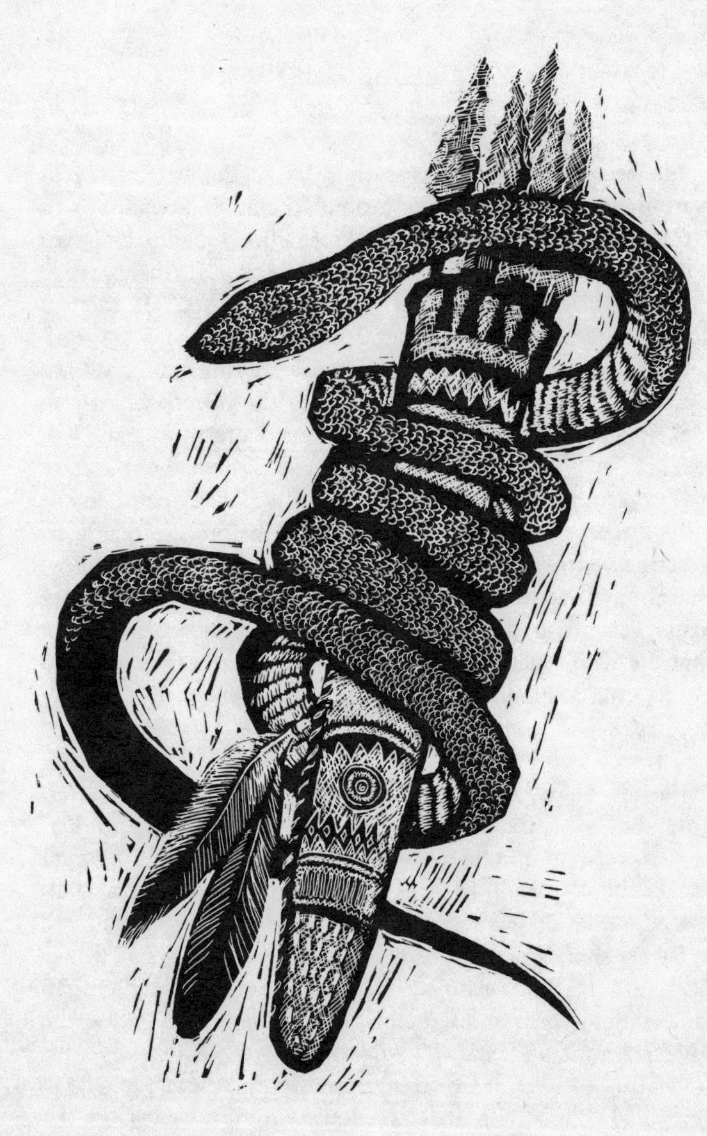

At once the men of Plymouth set to work putting up a stockade around their village, and set watches. For the moment, the Narragansets did not take up the challenge. In fact, they refused to accept the bullet-filled snakeskin, but sent it back.

By spring of the following year, the Englishmen were forced to conclude that one of their earliest Indian friends was playing them false.

> They begane to see that Squanto sought his own ends, and plaid his owne game, by putting the Indians in fear, and drawing gifts from them to enrich him selfe; making them believe he could stur up warr against whom he would, and make peece for whom he would. Yea, he made them believe they [the English] kept the plague buried in the ground, and could send it amongst whom they would, which did much terrifie the Indians, and made them depend more on him, and seeke more to him then to Massasoyte, which procured him envie, and had like to cost him his life. For after the discovery of his practises, Massasoyt sought it both privately and openly; which caused him to stick close to the English, and never durst goe from them till he dyed.... [Bradford]

In addition, the Englishmen resorted at this point to a bit of trickery, if we are to believe Bradford's account. They played on the enmity between Hobbomok, thoroughly loyal to Massasoit, and Squanto, "which made them cary more squarely. And the Govr seemed to countenance the one [Squanto] and the Captaine the other [Hobbomok], by which they had better intelligence, and made them both more diligente. . . ."

In spite of these tricks and countertricks, matters soon came to a head. One day the Pilgrims decided to make another journey into the country of the Massachusets to engage in further trading. Standish and his party, which included Squanto and Hobbomok, were barely out of sight in the shallop when an Indian, a friend of Squanto, came running toward the village, blood on his face. He claimed to have been at Nemasket, but had managed to get away, though he still gave the impression that pursuers were behind him.

He warned that Corbitant and the Narragansets, and probably Massasoit, were on their way to attack them.

Governor Bradford immediately assembled the military companies, and ordered the cannon fired to call back the shallop. It soon returned, with Hobbomok assuring them that the whole thing was a hoax. He himself was one of Massasoit's councillors, and would have been informed were any such treachery planned. He also sent his wife to Massasoit's headquarters to learn what was going on. While he did not openly accuse Squanto of being the author of the hoax, he had previously warned the Pilgrims that Squanto was plotting some mischief, apparently with the Narragansets and Massachusets.

Hobbomok's wife found nothing untoward being planned by the Wampanoags, but when she told Massasoit of the goings-on at Plymouth, he went into a rage at Squanto and his schemes. He appeared at Plymouth and demanded that Squanto be turned over to him, in the words of Edward Winslow's *Good News from New England,* "as being one of his subjects, whom by our first articles of peace we could not retain."

That put Bradford in a quandary. He knew very well that Massasoit was well within his rights in demanding Squanto according to Article II of the peace treaty. Furthermore, he himself was convinced that Squanto hoped by his tricks to depose Massasoit and himself take over as Grand Sachem. Nevertheless, Squanto had been their friend, and Bradford could not quite bring himself to send him to what doubtless would be his death.

He temporized by convincing Massasoit that Squanto had already been given a thorough tongue-lashing, and the Grand Sachem left to return home. He did not long remain convinced; his fury returned, and he sent back a messenger to Bradford, asking him "to give way to the death of Tisquantum, who had so much abused him."

This time Bradford was forced to admit that Squanto deserved death at the hands of Massasoit, but he begged the Grand Sachem not to take away "their tongue." This did not change the mind of Massasoit. Next time the messenger returned, a number of braves in war paint were with him.

They also brought along beaver pelts, and Massasoit's long knife. They had been told by the sachem to use this to cut off Squanto's "head and hands and bring them to him," and offered the beaver pelts in exchange.

Bradford managed to delay a little longer by assuring them that, "It is not the manner of the English to sell men's lives at a price." But by now he had run out of excuses. Squanto was called forth and gave himself up to Bradford's mercy, meanwhile blaming Hobbomok as "the author and worker of his overthrow."

At this point a new excuse intervened. According to Winslow, "at the instant when our governour was ready to deliver him into the hands of his executioners, a boat was seen at sea to cross before our town, and fall behind a head-land not far off. Whereupon, having heard many rumours of the French, and not knowing whether there were any combination between the Savages and them, the governour told the Indians, he would first know what boat that was, ere he would deliver him into their custody. But being mad with rage and impatient at delay, they departed in great heat."

Their heat was no greater than that of Massasoit when they brought the word to him. His friendship for the Pilgrims cooled and his anger mounted, and for quite a while thereafter he did not cease to frown on them. The strain eased four months later in September of 1622 when Squanto, accompanying some of the Englishmen on a trip around the Cape in search of corn, fell sick and died of an "Indean feavor" at Chatham. (The trip had been taken in aid of Thomas Weston's men, about whom there is more in a moment.)

The Pilgrims managed thereafter to survive without Squanto. Nevertheless, despite all their excuses for delay, it can hardly be denied that in failing to turn him over to Massasoit, they were the first to break the treaty of friendship and trust made only the year before. In fact, they were the only ones to break it during the lifetime of Massasoit.

The mysterious boat whose appearance provided Bradford his last excuse for delay, incidentally, proved to be manned by Englishmen. These "friends" would, in the end, cause them more trouble than had Squanto at his worst.

"WESTON'S RUDE FELLOWS"

In their first year and ten months at Plymouth, the Pilgrims had not fared too badly, thanks in part to their own industry and courage, but largely to the kindness and friendliness of Massasoit and his men. They had put up several crude houses and had planted Indian corn and some English grains as well, though the latter gave them a poor crop. They had established friendly relations with the majority of the Indians around them—again in large part due to the influence of Massasoit, and of the power his friendship gave to them. Here too, Squanto had played his part.

At the same time, they never seemed to have an abundance of food, and they had not been able to pay back any of their debt to the merchant adventurers of London, who had given them their financial backing for the venture. They had succeeded in loading one ship with beaver pelts and the like, but the ship was waylaid by French pirates off the coast of England, and all the valuable cargo seized.

Thus the merchant adventurers were not happy. One of them, Thomas Weston, washed his hands of the whole business, left the company and began to operate on his own. The trouble with the Pilgrims, he reasoned, was that many of them had brought their wives to America with them, and were too busy taking care of them and their children to spend the necessary amount of time in trading with the Indians for furs. Therefore he and his son Andrew toured the taverns and coffeehouses of London and chose a group of young single men to send to America to set up a colony which would produce riches for its backers.

These men, or an advance party of them, were those the Pilgrims had seen in the mystery boat. They soon spotted the little settlement at Plymouth and came ashore.

The Pilgrims had had ample warning of them. Robert Cushman wrote: "Mr. Weston hath quite broken of our company. . . . The people which they carry are no men for us, wherfore I pray you entertaine them not, neither exchange man for man with them, excepte it be some of our worst. . . . If they borrow anything of you, let them leave a good pawne. . . ." And John Peirce, in the same vein, said: "But as for Mr. Weston's company, I think them so base in condition (for the most parte) as in all apearance not fitt for an honest mans company. . . ." Even Weston himself told the Pilgrims: "Now I will not deney but ther are many of our people rude fellows . . . yet I presume they will be governed by such as I set over them. . . ." He also promised to send a sizeable amount of bread in his ship, but the ship arrived without it, and his men with little food and not much more than the clothes on their backs.

Thus they came ashore looking for food and shelter, of which the Pilgrims had little enough for themselves, while their ship sailed on to Virginia. Yet in spite of this and of the warnings about Weston's men, the Pilgrims, according to Bradford, "concluded to give his men frendly entertainmente . . . partly in compassion to the people, who were now come into a wilderness (as themselves were) . . . and they were alltogeather unacquainted & knew not what to doe. So . . . they . . . received these (being aboute 60. lusty men), and gave housing for them selves and their goods; and many being sicke, they had the best means the place could afford them."

They remained at Plymouth for most of the summer, then when the ship that had brought them returned from Virginia, they "removed into Massachusset Bay [to Wessagusset, now Weymouth] . . . . Yet they left all their sicke folke hear till they were settled and housed. But of ther victuals they had not any, though they were in great wante, nor any thing els in recompence of any courtecie done them; neither did they [the Pilgrims] desire it, for they saw they were an unruly company, and had no good governmente over them, and by disorder would soon fall into wants if Mr. Weston came not the sooner amongst them; and therefore, to prevente all after occasion, would have nothing of them. . . ." [Bradford]

Unfortunately, the Pilgrims did not long hold to this wise

resolve. They were far from being rid of "Weston's rude fellows." A few months later, in February of 1622, a messenger came to Plymouth from John Sanders, now their "cheefe," telling of "the great wants they were falen into." The 26 or 28 hogsheads of corn and beans they had gotten on their trip to the Cape were long since gone; they had tried to borrow more from the Massachuset Indians, but the latter refused them. Now Sanders proposed to take it by force, first asking if the Governor of Plymouth approved.

The Governor was understandably horrified, and tried to dissuade Sanders, all the Pilgrim leaders signing a protest. Already Weston's men had stolen some of the Indians' corn, and this act would no doubt bring retaliation not only upon the Massachusetts Bay colony, but upon Plymouth as well. After all, the Massachuset Indians had never been overly friendly, even to the men of Plymouth.

Apparently Sanders was dissuaded, but this did not prevent some of his men, according to Bradford, from telling the Indians "that their Govr was purposed to come and take their corne by force. The which with other things made them enter into a conspiracie against the English. . . ."

Weston's men were probably a worthless lot, as unsuited as a baby to life in the wilderness. They were not much disposed to hard work, and when they had food they wasted it. Eventually some sold their clothes and bed coverings. Others "became servants to the Indians, and would cutt them woode and fetch them water, for a cap full of corne; others fell to plaine stealing, both night & day from the Indeans, of which they greevosly complained." Some died of cold and hunger, others left their houses and scattered up and down the coast, looking for food. The Indians scorned and insulted them, and even snatched such food as they had from their cooking pots and took their blankets off them while they slept and made off with them.

It must not be forgotten that these accounts all come from the Pilgrims. Evidence to the contrary is understandably scanty, but it does appear that Weston's men got on somewhat better with the Indians than the Pilgrim accounts would lead us to believe. At least, they did manage to carry on some trade in furs with them, which did not please the

men of Plymouth. Quite possibly Bradford and the rest exaggerated, for they heartily disapproved of these "godless" people from the start. Godless, that is, as far as the Separatist views of the Pilgrims were concerned. Such religion as Weston's men possessed was that of the Church of England, the Anglican creed.

At this delicate point in the proceedings, Captain Standish made a trip by shallop to the Cape, where he spread his own peculiar brand of goodwill. A short time before, Bradford had gone there with some of Weston's men to buy corn and beans and succeeded in getting more than could be carried back in the ship. What was left over had been left piled on the beach, with a promise from Aspinet, the Nauset sachem, from Canacum of Manomet (Bourne), and from Iyanough of Cummaquid that the food would remain unharmed. All of these men, according to Bradford, had been very friendly and had gone out of their way to provide the Pilgrims with the grain, some of which they could hardly spare.

The Indians had kept their promises. On the beach at Nauset Standish found the supplies intact, but on their shallop which had been damaged on the previous trip and left on the beach, some beads, scissors, and other trifles left there were gone. The short-tempered Standish roared off with a party of men under arms to confront Aspinet and there demanded that the trifles be returned at once, "or else he would revenge it on them before his departure. . . ."

Aspinet, astonished by such rude behavior, the next morning appeared at the beach, "accompanied with many men, in a stately manner." He apologized profusely, returned the stolen trifles, and assured Standish that the man who stole them had been "much beaten." He also gave the Englishmen some tasty, freshly-baked corn bread.

Apparently not in the least mollified, Standish sailed on to Cummaquid and virtually repeated the procedure—and this time after Iyanough and his men had brought the Pilgrims in out of a violent blizzard to spend the night in their huts as guests. The Cummaquids, like the Nausets, had carefully guarded the visitors' store of corn, but once again Standish missed some of his "trifles." At once he stamped up to the village, surrounded the hut of Iyanough with his musketeers, and demanded that his trinkets be given back to him, "threatening to fall upon them without further delay if they would not forthwith restore them."

The astounded Iyanough came out and gently asked the Captain to "search whether they were not about the boat." When this was done the beads were found, "lying openly on the boat's cuddy." Standish did not trouble to apologize for his outrageous conduct; he was convinced that the thief had slipped down and put them back. The Cummaquid were merely "pretending their wonted love."

After a short time Standish went back to the Cape, to Manomet. The sachem there was Canacum, who had so favorably impressed Bradford not long before. He did not impress Standish; the captain was angry at "not finding the entertainment he found elsewhere, and the Governor had here received."

As Willison points out in *Saints and Strangers,* it is quite possible that Canacum had received word of the goings-on at Nauset and Cummaquid, and perhaps did not care for the role of kindly host to this man. Furthermore, the word of Sanders' proposed attack at Wessagusset had undoubtedly reached the Cape by now. As far as the Cape Indians knew, the men of the two settlements were partners. They had come on a trip to the Cape together, and had lived together for some time. If Sanders meant to rob the Indians of food by force, wouldn't the men of Plymouth join him? It was hardly a time for extending the warm hand of friendship, especially to a man like Standish.

The captain soon found other reasons for his anger. In walked two Indians from Wessagusset! One of them was Wituwamat, a "notable insulting villain," a Massachuset and a Pinese, or Panese. This, in their language, signified a strong man, a man of valor, and it was believed that a Pinese could not be killed in battle. This one did not think highly of white men, it appears, as he "derided their weakness, especially because, as he said, they died crying, making sour faces, more like children than men." On top of this, Wituwamet's "entertainment much exceeded the Captain's," which made Standish so furious with his hosts that he "scorned at their behavior, and told them of it."

Nor was this all that the thin-skinned, short tempered captain had to suffer. Wituwamet drew out a long knife, gave it to Canacum, and proceeded to speak at length "in an audacious manner, framing it in such sort as the Captain, though he be the best linguist amongst us, could not gather anything from it."

It even seems safe to hazard a guess at this point—though it can only be a guess—that just perhaps Wituwamet, like most Indians, possessed a sense of humor and was having a bit of fun at the captain's expense. If so, in the long run it would prove a tragic joke for Wituwamet, for he was dealing with a man who was utterly devoid of humor and seemed never to have forgotten an insult.

Assuredly Standish was not the best linguist among them and apparently he had no interpreter with him, but in spite of that he claimed to have "afterward discovered" the substance of Wituwamet's speech to Canacum. The Massachusets were planning to wipe out Weston's colony at Wessagusset, and since they were afraid that the Pilgrims at Plymouth would never leave the death of their countrymen unrevenged, they wanted the Cape tribes to join them in an attack on Plymouth. They could not be successful "without the overthrow of both Plantations."

If this were the plan, why did they not attack Standish and his party at this point?

To add a bit more salt to the savoury dish he was cooking up—if indeed he was—Standish told also of a Pamet Indian who came in that evening, and who in the past had been "very affable, courteous, and loving, especially towards the Captain." He still was, or seemed so, but now Standish decided that this friendly attitude was all deceit, a part of the plot to murder him in his sleep. In spite of this, the Pamet was allowed to spend the night at the Pilgrim camp, but the captain outwitted this fiend by staying awake and on his feet all night! Not only that, but Standish took him along to Plymouth next day. He even planned a trip with the Pamet to the Cape for more corn, but was prevented by a storm. Thus, if we are to believe Standish, the dastardly plan to murder him was foiled a second time.

Perhaps this is unduly skeptical of the doughty captain. Nevertheless, this account of events nicely set the stage for what would soon occur—a thing which Standish, and probably many of the Pilgrims, had desired for some time—the liquidation of Weston's colony, and the cowing of the Massachuset Indians. These two annoyances would be taken care of at one blow.

STANDISH'S TRICKERY

Meanwhile, back at Plymouth Plantation, word came that Massasoit was very sick and near death. Immediately young Edward Winslow, whom Massasoit considered his good friend, set out with Hobbomok for Sowams. On the way, in one of Corbitant's villages, an old woman told them that Massasoit was already dead. At the news, according to Winslow, Hobbomok cried out,*"Neen womasu Sagimus, neen womasu Sagimus!* [My loving sachem, my loving sachem!] Many have I known, but never any like thee." And to Winslow: "Whilst you live, you will never see his like among the Indians. He was no liar. He was not cruel and bloody like other Indians. In anger and passion he was soon cooled, easy to be reconciled towards such as had offended him, ruled by reason in such measure as he would not scorn the advice of mean men and governed his men better with a few strokes than others did with many, truly loving where he loved. Yea! I fear you have not a faithful friend left among the Indians."

Winslow and Hobbomok hurried on through the dark forest, arriving at Sowams late that night. Happily they found the rumor false. Massasoit was very ill, and had lost his sight, but he still lived. When informed of Winslow's arrival, he took his hand and said, "O Winsnow, [Winslow] I shall never see thee again!"

But Winslow had carried with him "a confection of many comfortable conserves," and with the permission of the powwows who surrounded the Grand Sachem, he administered them. In time sight returned to Massasoit. Within a day or two, with further ministrations, he was up and about again and assuring his people that, "Now I see the English are my friends and love me, and whilst I live, I will never forget this kindness they have showed me."

Indian Tribes and Confederations in MASSACHUSETTS & RHODE ISLAND

INDIAN TRIBES OR CONFEDERATIONS IN CAPITAL LETTERS

TOWNS IN ITALIC LETTERS

UNDERLINED TOWNS HIT OR DESTROYED IN KING PHILIP'S WAR

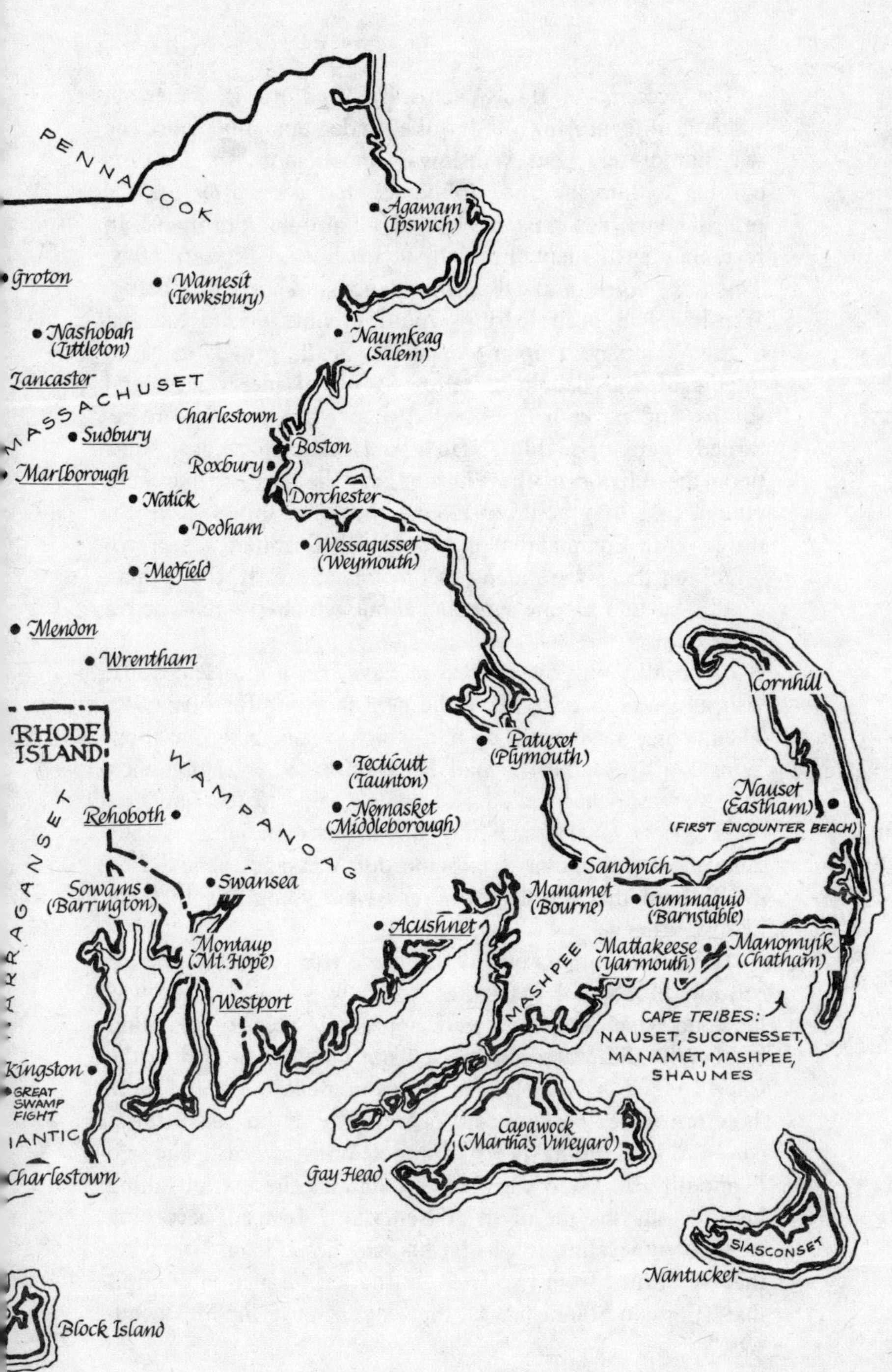

PENNACOOK
Agawam
(Ipswich)
Groton
Wamesit
(Tewksbury)
Nashobah
(Littleton)
Naumkeag
(Salem)
Lancaster
MASSACHUSET
Charlestown
Sudbury
Boston
Roxbury
Marlborough
Natick
Dorchester
Dedham
Wessagusset
(Weymouth)
Medfield
Mendon
Wrentham
Cornhill
RHODE
ISLAND
Patuxet
(Plymouth)
WAMPANOAG
Tecticutt
(Taunton)
Nauset
(Eastham)
Nemasket
(Middleborough)
Rehoboth
(FIRST ENCOUNTER BEACH)
NARRAGANSET
Sandwich
Sowams
(Barrington)
Swansea
Manamet
(Bourne)
Cummaquid
(Barnstable)
Acushnet
Montaup
(Mt. Hope)
Mattakeese
(Yarmouth)
Manomyik
(Chatham)
MASHPEE
Westport
CAPE TRIBES:
NAUSET, SUCONESSET,
MANAMET, MASHPEE,
SHAUMES
Kingston
GREAT
SWAMP
FIGHT
Capawock
(Martha's Vineyard)
NIANTIC
Charlestown
Gay Head
SIASCONSET
Nantucket
Block Island

The account of these events by Bradford is somewhat vague and confusing, and quite understandably, since he was not present; but Winslow is much more specific. According to him, he and Hobbomok left soon after for the return home, accompanied by, of all people, Corbitant! In fact, they even spent the night in his hut on Buzzard's Bay. This *bête noire* of the Pilgrims, whom a short time before Winslow had been fearing would become Grand Sachem of the Wampanoag upon Massasoit's death, proved to be an intelligent and delightful fellow, "full of merry jests and squibs, and never better pleased than when the like are returned again upon him." He asked many questions, some upon the religion of the Pilgrims, and he and his men concluded that they believed almost the same things, save for the Seventh Commandment with which Corbitant disagreed, "thinking there were many inconveniences in it, that a man should be tied to one woman, about which we reasoned a good while."

All in all, Winslow seemed to have had a most enjoyable visit and was sorry to leave the next morning for Plymouth. Then comes a statement by him which is somewhat puzzling. Winslow writes that he had been informed by Hobbomok that Massasoit had called Hobbomok aside to tell him that the Pilgrims must attack the Massachuset Indians, as they planned at any moment to wipe out Wessagusset and Plymouth, and that the Cape Indians were going to join them in this little war!

As Willison points out, if this were true, why had Massasoit told Hobbomok instead of Winslow, since Winslow was his good friend and they were apparently able to communicate? Why did Massasoit himself not take action against the Cape Indians, who belonged to his confederation and were therefore under his authority? And why, if he had just received this alarming news, did not Winslow rush back to Plymouth at once to warn the inhabitants, instead of taking his time, staying the night at Nemasket? Instead, according to his own account, it was on his way home from Nemasket that he learned from two friendly Indians he met on the trail that "Captain Standish was, that day, gone to the Massachusets."

In other words, if there ever had been such a plot hatched, Plymouth did not learn of it from Massasoit by way of Winslow. And this leads Willison to the conclusion, which I am inclined to accept, that the story of Massasoit's warning was cooked up afterward, to justify Standish's outrageous actions on the Cape and his subsequent ones at Wessagusset. Certainly they needed justification.

Arriving at Wessagusset with Hobbomok and eight other men armed to the teeth, Standish reported the deplorable conditions he had expected to find—Weston's men "senseless of their own miserie." Their vessel, the *Swan*, lay empty and unguarded in the harbor. The captain and his crew were ashore, gathering clams and groundnuts. When they finally appeared, Standish asked them how they dared expose themselves to such danger.

"We fear not the Indians," was their answer, "but live with them and suffer them to lodge with us, not having sword or gun, or needing none."

"If there is no cause, I am the gladder," snorted Standish.

He then went on to see Governor Sanders and tell him of his plans. Sanders and his men protested but finally gave in. For a few days Standish put on his most deceitful manner and engaged in trading for furs with the Massachusets, but his deceits did not fool anyone. Pecksuot, a powerful man, came in and told Hobbomok that he was aware Standish meant to attack them.

"Tell him we know it, but fear him not. Neither will we shun him, but let him begin when he dare." And to Standish a little later: "Though you are a great captain, yet you are but a little man, and though I be no sachem, yet I am a man of great strength and courage."

Wituwamet also came to indulge in his own special brand of Standish-baiting, producing a long knife with the handle carved in the likeness of a woman's face.

"I have another at home, bearing a man's face, wherewith I have killed both French and English," he announced, "and by and by the two must marry."

These two were marked down by Standish for his first vengeance against their insults. They were lured to Pilgrim headquarters, under the pretext, some say, of being invited to a feast. Along with them came another brave and Wituwamet's young brother, whose age is variously stated as fifteen and eighteen.

Once they were inside the building, someone fastened the door and Standish attacked Pecksuot, killing him with the Indian's own knife. After a fierce struggle in which the Indians fought bravely and well, sustaining many wounds, Wituwamet and the other brave were slain by Standish's men. Only the boy remained unharmed, and Standish promptly had him hanged from the rafters in the room where his brother had been killed.

The captain then gave orders to Weston's men and to his own to kill every Indian warrior to be found in the village, but they only managed to get three, in spite of the fact that the attack had caught the Indians by surprise. One got away, and the rest were women, who were merely rounded up. Then Standish and his men marched out of town, "still seek-to make spoil of them and theirs." A band of the Massachusets fired arrows at them from the cover of the trees, but slowly retreated and found security in a swamp where even Standish did not wish to follow.

Back in the village, the captain met with Weston's men and "offered to bring them hither [to Plymouth] if they thought good . . . till Mr. Weston or some supplie came to them." But most of them preferred to "goe with their smale ship to the eastward, wher hapily they might here of Mr. Weston, or some supply from him, seing the time of the year was for fishing ships to be in the land. . . . So they shipped what they had of any worth, and he got them all the corne he could . . . and saw them well out of the bay, under saile at sea, and so came home. . . ." [Bradford]

Thus with one stroke Standish disposed of both Weston's colony (with their threat to the beaver trade) and the Massachuset Indians. Weston's men were never heard of again and quite possibly were lost at sea on the way to the fishing fleet off the coast of Maine or Nova Scotia. The Massachuset Indians would not prove a serious threat to the Pilgrims again. If, indeed, they ever had. Thomas Morton, admittedly no friend or admirer of the self-styled Saints, said after some years of experience with these Indians, "I have found the Massachusets Indians more full of humanitie than the Christians, and have had much better quarter with them."

Indirectly, Standish also succeeded, by reason of his dealings at Wessagusset, in disposing of those Indian sachems who had treated the Pilgrims in the most friendly fashion. When word of his latest foray reached the Cape, these "forsook their houses, running to and fro like men distracted, living in swamps and other desert places." Men such as "grave" Canacum, "stately" Aspinet, and "gentle" Iyanough fell victims to the general terror. All eventually died in the swamps from fear, hunger or disease.

If in fact, as Standish claimed, these men had all along been in league with the Massachusets in plotting an attack upon the colonists, then this fear and eventual fate could have resulted from knowledge that their plot had been exposed. But it seems far more likely that it came from their recent experiences with the angry and obstreperous Standish. If he could treat the few and relatively powerless Massachuset men as he had, then obviously the Cape sachems were next on his list for extermination.

Unfortunately, we have no record of what Massasoit thought about the effect upon these sachems who belonged to his confederation and were therefore his friends and allies, but we do know what John Robinson thought. This truly saintly man, who had been the Pilgrim's highly respected pastor in Leyden and had longed ever since their leaving to join them there at Plymouth, got word of the doings at Wessagusset, and wrote:

> Concerning the killings of those poor Indians, oh! how happy a thing it had been if you had converted some before you killed any; besids, where blood is once shed, it is seldome stanched off a long time after . . . of your Captaine . . . there may be wanting that tenderness of the life of man (made after God's image) which is meete. . . .
>
> It is a thing more glorious in men's eyes than pleasing in God's, or conveniente for Christians, to be a terrour to poore barbarous people.

Thus ended, in the space of less than three years, the truly peaceful era in which the colonists could roam the forests at will, fearing no attack from hostile natives. The winter of 1622-23 found the Pilgrims somewhat hungry, since they feared to forage in the woods as they had in the past. But they could hardly have suffered as those sachems of the Cape had suffered, for the Pilgrims did not "die in the swamps."

ENGLISHMEN, ENGLISHMEN!

Many of these pages have tended to show the Pilgrim forefathers in rather a poor light. Since my purpose is to hunt down the truth wherever it can be found, rather than to defame any one group of people in particular, perhaps it is time to say a few words in defense of those Pilgrims—or Separatists, or "Brownists," as they are sometimes called. In the first place, they were poor people for the most part, and would never have reached America had they not been backed by the merchant adventurers.

These businessmen constantly cheated them, and it was a long time before they could repay their debt. They often went hungry and lacked necessary supplies. During these years visitors to New England, men not of their faith, took back to England countless highly unfavorable reports of the colony, some true but many of them slanderous. Against such reports, it seemed vital to the Pilgrims to keep the knowledge of any mistakes they made from reaching their backers. Thus, presumably, the apparent attempt to explain away the affair at Wessagusset.

This affair seems to have been largely the doing of Myles Standish, not the Pilgrims. Standish, as mentioned before, was not one of them, but rather one of the "Strangers." A former lieutenant in the war in the Netherlands, he went aboard at Plymouth and came to America presumably for adventure and profit. He was doubtless made welcome as the only man among them with military experience—experience they feared would be needed.

He did prove to be a good fighting man, but he was no diplomat, and diplomacy might well have been more useful than prowess in battle against the usually peaceful Indians of the area. His face could flare almost as red as his hair when he was angry, and it seems he was angry a good deal

of the time—especially when confronted with Indians. The Pilgrims had chosen him as their military leader and so were responsible for his acts. He never did join their church, yet he seemingly received all the privileges normally given only to church members. This increased the responsibility of the Pilgrims.

Aside from this error of judgment, or act of necessity if one prefers, the Pilgrims' treatment of the Indians in those early days was somewhat more in keeping with their own idea of themselves as followers in God's ways. At least one writer has gone so far as to say that they thought of the Indians simply as fellow sinners under God's heaven. This appears to be putting it rather strongly, but certainly their attitude was a distinct improvement over that of the sharp traders and ship captains who had preceeded them, and probably better than that of the white men who would come in succeeding generations.

It must also be remembered that the Pilgrims were but few in number, and the settlement at Plymouth never did become a large one. Whatever their inclinations with respect to the Indians, the "Saints" numbered a few score as against thousands of Indians, and it behooved them to have as peaceful relations as possible. This, aside from the angry excursions of Standish, they generally did. In addition, their settlement was upon land bereft of its original inhabitants by the plague, and for some time they did not require much room for expansion. When they did acquire any, it was normally from friendly Indians who welcomed the presence of this little band of white men.

Then, within the space of a few years, the picture changed. More Englishmen, pouring into the land, settled around Massachusetts Bay and later inland! It began in 1629, when six ships came into the harbor at Naumkeag (Salem) and unloaded supplies and men. Soon after these settlers removed to what they considered a better spot in Boston Harbor, at the present site of Charlestown. The next year, ten more ships arrived, and this flood of settlers continued for ten years. By that time, numbering around forty thousand, the English population probably outnumbered the entire Indian population of all New England.

Unlike the Pilgrims, these second-comers were not poor tradesmen and artisans who came to America with little more than the clothes on their backs. Most of them were well-to-do, and they brought with them a great deal in the way of supplies and possessions. These included cattle and horses, which meant that they were going to need a great deal of land. This meant more trouble for the Indians. They soon began to acquire that land, spreading about the harbor and well inland. After all, hadn't King James, indirectly through Sir Ferdinando Gorges and his "Council for New England," granted them a strip of land that stretched all across the continent, from coast to coast? Of course, they usually paid the Indians for the land, at trifling cost to themselves, but that did not alter the fact that soon there would be no room for the Indian to live his own kind of life in the area.

These men were Puritans. In England they had spurned the Separatist doctrine of the Pilgrims, maintaining that they did not wish to separate from the Church of England, but only to reform or purify it. That was a safer doctrine to hold in England, particularly if you were a man of property. But in this new land, far from the clutches of the Archbishop of Canterbury, they soon had a change of heart. They embraced the Pilgrims as brothers and soon began preaching Separatism. Thus the two colonies, Massachusetts Bay and Plymouth, presented a united front to the outnumbered Indians.

The Indians soon began to feel the effect of all this. Within a decade, not only had the recent settlers spread out all around Boston, but northward as far as Merrimac near the border of what is now New Hampshire, and into New Hampshire itself at Pascataquack (Exeter) and Winicowett (Hampton). They had begun to settle along the Connecticut River, as far north as Hartford, and then even to Quinnipiac (New Haven). Others, principally Pilgrims, set up plantations at Sandwich and Mattakeese (Yarmouth) on Cape Cod.

Thus the Indian land began to dribble away. Eventually Roger Williams protested to Governor Bradford of Plymouth that "James has no more right to give away or sell Massasoit's lands and cut and carve his country than Massasoit has to sell King James' kingdom or to send Indians to colonize Warwickshire." But then, Bradford considered Williams "a man godly and zealous, having many precious parts, but very unsettled in judgemente" and so perhaps did not take his words too seriously. Williams by now had been forced to leave Massachusetts because of disputes over church doctrine, and he set up his own colony in Rhode Island.

As I have pointed out, it is certainly true that in most instances the colonists bought the land from the Indians rather than seizing it outright. In some cases the Indians did not quite realize what they were doing, thinking that they were only giving the white man the right to roam the land at will, as they themselves had done in the past. In other instances, they undoubtedly understood quite well, or at least the sachems who made the agreements did. Sometimes they did so under the influence of white man's liquor, or they did it for personal gain, for a sachem who did not have enough wealth to give presents to his people at appropriate times would not have been highly respected. (There is even some question as to whether, by Indian custom, a sachem had the right to sell the land of his tribe. Land was ordinarily gained by conquest, not by purchase.) At any rate, the land changed hands, probably in amounts so small by Indian standards as to cause little concern at first.

By the time it did, it was usually too late, although there was an occasional exception. In 1652, Mooanam or Wamsutta, eldest son of Massasoit, married the squaw sachem of the Pocassets, and began selling her land. Finally she resorted to the courts and stopped the practice.

English courts and English laws appeared not often to have provided justice for Indians, at least where it was a case of white versus Indian. True, Indians themselves often sat upon the juries, especially in the early days, but they seldom if ever fully understood the process of English law and justice. They thought it a shocking thing that a man should be condemned to a flogging. True, they themselves sometimes tortured prisoners, though it was done more often in anger rather than as a matter of common practice, as we have often been led to believe. But whipping was something else. It was a disgrace to the man who was whipped, a dishonorable thing.

Certainly the colonists attempted to dispense even-handed justice to white man and Indian alike, and no doubt believed that they were doing so. And there are examples to prove this. There was one Josiah Plaistowe, who, with his two servants was convicted of stealing corn from Chickataubut. The servants were whipped, twofold restitution ordered, and Plaistowe lost his rank of "gentleman"—no small thing in rank-conscious early America. This also deprived him of his privileges as a freeman and a voter. When Sir Richard Saltonstall's drunken servants burned the wigwams of Wonohaquaham, sachem of Winnisimmet, Saltonstall also paid, but he was not otherwise punished. In this case, of course, he was not himself involved in the crime.

But there was also the case of Walter Bagnall and Poquanam, which never reached the courts. Poquanam, sachem of Nahant, also known as Black Will, was a personable fellow and a good friend to the colonists with a penchant for wearing European clothes. In fact, one Thomas Dexter claimed that Poquanam had sold Nahant to Dexter for a suit of clothes. Poquanam denied this, and the case went to the courts. Before it was settled, in favor of Poquanam's people, Walter Bagnall entered the picture.

Bagnall was a servant of Thomas Morton, that *bete noire* of Pilgrim and Puritan alike, and Morton had set him up at a trading post on Richmond Isle in Casco Bay, Maine. There he promptly started cheating the Indians who came to trade with him. In 1631, the Casco Indians killed him and his assistant and burned his house.

The killing of a white man by Indians seldom went unpunished, but in this case Governor Winthrop of the Massachusetts Bay Colony refused to send soldiers against the Casco Indians, noting that Bagnall, "a wicked fellow," had "much wronged" them. However, the next year soldiers were sent north in ships on a hunt for pirates. They found no pirates, but they did find Poquanam fishing on Richmond Isle, took him and hanged him for the killing of Bagnall in which he had no part!

Governor Winthrop wrote of being shocked by the murder of Poquanam, but nothing whatsoever was done to the soldiers.

Once at least, in 1638, three white men were actually executed for robbing and murdering a Narraganset who strayed into their camp one evening. But these men had been fleeing the English to join with the Dutch to the west. Two of them, says Bradford, were "other men's servants and apprentices" escaping from bondage, and the third "was not only rune into debte, but he had gott a maid with child" and feared punishment. Furthermore, Roger Williams, a friend to the Narragansets, interceded on the side of justice, and in this case the Pilgrims apparently took his advice.

PLAGUES AND ALARMS

If white man's law and white man's greed for land proved a constant problem to the Indians, white man's diseases were a constant threat—even deadlier than his muskets. This time it was smallpox. It first appeared around the Dutch trading houses along the Connecticut River, in 1633, and then around the trading houses of the English in the same area. Soon it spread to Rhode Island and Massachusetts, and according to Winthrop, by 1634 "it was gone as far as any Indian plantation was known to the west." At Narragansett 700 died. Wonohaquanam, who first had his wigwams burned by whites, then his corn destroyed by English cattle, and since then had been fighting for his land in the courts, was one of the casualties. Most of his Massachuset tribesmen died as well, as many as thirty in a single day. Chickataubut, who, after an early brush with Standish and his men over the desecration of his mother's grave had been a good friend to the English, was also struck down. Many of the Wampanoag died.

> A sorer disease cannot befall them; they fear it more then the plague; for usualy they that have this disease have them in abundance, and .. fall into a lamentable condition ... and dye like rotten sheep. The condition of this people was so lamentable ... as they were (in the end) not able to help one another, no, not to make a fire, nor to fetch a little water to drinke, nor to burie the dead.... But .. the English ... had compastion of them, and dayly fetched them wood & water, and made them fires, gott them victualls whilst they lived, and buried them when they dyed.... But by the marvelous goodnes & providense of God not one of the English was so much as sicke... And this mercie which they shewed them was kindly taken.... [Bradford]

This account of Bradford's relates to the smallpox in Connecticut, but much the same was true when the disease struck the parent colonies to the east. Here again, many of the English ministered to the stricken Indians, notably one Samuel Maverick. Orphaned Indian children were adopted into English homes, although most of them later died. And no doubt this mercy was "kindly taken," although the smallpox itself had been a gift of the white man.

In the long run, of course, the lessening of the Indian population as a result of the smallpox served further to strengthen the hand of the colonists, already growing strong. There were constant "alarums and excursions," rumors of Indian plots against the whites, most of them only rumors. Here is one which, if the actual events were correctly related in Winthrop's *Journal,* must have contained more than a kernel of truth. He speaks of a "broil between their men [Plymouth's] at Sowams and the Narragansets, who set upon the English house there to have taken Owsamequin [Massasoit] the sagamore of Packanocutt who fled thither with all his people for refuge; and . . . Captain Standish, being gone thither to relieve the three English, which were in the house, had sent home in all haste for more men and other provisions, upon intelligence that Canonicus, with a great army, was coming against them." More powder, at least, was sent to him, but by the time it arrived, the Narragansets had left to fight with their long-time enemies, the Pequots of Connecticut.

Was this attack on the English house just a passing diversion on the way to more serious business? We don't know. Generally speaking, Canonicus and his Narragansets, ever since the exchange of a bundle of shot for a bundle of arrows, had maintained peaceful relations with the English. But it is true that they bore no love for Massasoit.

Nevertheless, in the mid-1630s real trouble loomed ahead, not with the Narragansets but westward in Connecticut. As previously mentioned, settlers from Massachusetts moved into the Connecticut River valley, established themselves at Wethersfield and elsewhere in the present Hartford area, and even built a fort at Saybrook. Originally they were invited in by the local sachems as a protective measure against the Pequot or Mohegan-Pequot Indians who, not many years before, had themselves moved into Connecticut. They were a warlike people with a love for conquest and before long had established domain over most of the Connecticut Indians. These subjugated tribes, once free, had since been chafing under their harsh jurisdiction.

The coming of the English would indeed bring an end to Pequot rule, but would eventually result in a more destructive one. Trouble for the English began in 1633 when a dissolute trader, one Captain Stone, was killed on the river by Pequots, and his ship and crew blown up by an explosion of powder. There were various versions of this affair, but the most likely one is that Stone was killed in revenge for the recent murder by Dutch traders of the Grand Sachem of the Pequot nation. It is probable, as the Pequots claimed, that they could not tell a Dutchman from an Englishman. To an Indian, all white men looked alike.

But to the English, even if the killing had been justified, what mattered was that a white man had been killed by Indians. There must be punishment.

Sassacus, now Grand Sachem of the Pequot, was still fighting the Dutch. He did not wish at this point to take on the English as well. He settled with the English for a treaty of sorts, which provided for the payment of wampum and handing over of Stone's killers to the English. In return, the English promised to send him ships with goods for trade. But neither side did much to carry out its part of the treaty.

Then, in 1636, Indians on Block Island killed a second white trader, the "notorious" and "turbulent" John Oldham. He was probably killed by Narragansets, but the Massachusetts Bay authorities accused the Pequots of harboring the killers and taking part in the crime. They raised a company of ninety men, placed them under the command of John Endicott, and prepared to give the Pequots a taste of English justice.

But their actions served only to show Sassacus that the English were afraid to fight. They went from Block Island to the mouth of the Pequot (Thames) River, laying waste to a few hundred acres of Indian corn, burning a few wigwams, destroying canoes—and perhaps killing two Indians!

Then they sailed back to Boston, not having lost a man.

Winslow, governor of Plymouth, assessed the situation in a letter to John Winthrop, deputy governor of the Massachusetts Bay Colony, accusing him of having "occasioned a war, etc., by provoking the Pequods, and no more. . . ." Winthrop "took it ill, (as there was reason) and returned answer accordingly. . . ."

Despite Winthrop's anger, Winslow proved right. And his words were but an echo of those of Lieutenant Lion Gardiner, commander of the fort at Saybrook, who assured Endicott that he had but stirred up a hornet's nest about the ears of the settlers of Connecticut, leaving them to incur the stings. They soon did.

Apparently Sassacus had by now concluded that the time had come to attack the English before they grew too numerous to fight. Furthermore, Endicott's fumbling expedition had convinced him that they were not a courageous lot. First he sent emissaries to the Narraganset, with whom he was now at peace, hoping to make an alliance with them. He would probably have succeeded had it not been for Roger Williams who, at the request of the Massachusetts authorities, interceded in time to prevent the alliance.

Then Sassacus moved without the Narraganset. There were attacks on the men of Gardiner's fort when they were outside the walls and attacks upon traders who ventured up the river in spite of Gardiner's warnings. Soon an excuse for open warfare came.

It was provided by Sowheag, sachem of the Wangunks, or rather, by the colonists who had broken their word to him. Once he had turned to the English for protection against Sassacus; now he turned to Sassacus for protection against the English.

Sassacus was glad to oblige. Two hundred Pequot sannops (braves) slipped through the forest in April of 1637 and fell upon the settlement at Wethersfield. They killed six men and three women, captured two teen-aged girls, slaughtered cattle and damaged property. Then the forest once more swallowed them.

The Pequot War had begun. The little Connecticut colony raised an "army" of ninety men and placed them under the command of Captain John Mason. The Bay Colony sent nineteen under Captain John Underhill and promised two hundred more. Plymouth had taken rather a dim view of these proceedings from the start, but John Winthrop, Jr., governor of the Connecticut colony and son of the Massachusetts Winthrop, wrote an appeal to Bradford, noting that "withall we conceive that you looke upon the Pequots, *and all other Indians,* [italics mine] as a commone enimie." Plymouth finally promised to raise fifty men but did not succeed in doing so.

Mason also had an Indian ally in Uncas, a Pequot who now called himself a Mohegan. Uncas had left the Pequot tribe after his rather dubious claim to the grand sachemship was denied. Along with some of his relatives and other disaffected tribesmen he set up his own group. Now anxious for revenge and to prove himself the white man's friend, he joined Mason's army with 70 warriors.

Rhode Island, which had two colonies, one the Providence Plantations and the other on Aquidneck Island (now Rhode Island) in Narraganset Bay, furnished no men and probably was not asked to do so. After all, these two colonies were filled with dissenters from the Puritan and Pilgrim faiths,and so not suitable allies. The Bay authorities did, however, ask advice from Roger Williams. Since this expedition was not against his friends the Narragansets, he willingly gave it. It was not always followed.

Mason, taking ship at Saybrook, wisely bypassed the center of Pequot activities at Pequot Harbor (New London) and sailed on to Narragansett Bay. He asked permission of Miantinomo to go through Narraganset territory, and the latter willingly granted it. (Miantinomo, nephew of Grand Sachem Canonicus, seems by now to have been Acting Grand Sachem, for his uncle had grown old.)

A few Narragansets joined with Mason. Later, as he marched through their territory, several Eastern Nehantics joined. They went westward to the Mystic River, crossed it, and before dawn fell upon the Pequot fort in West Mystic, catching its defenders by surprise. They attacked first with sword and musket, then set fire to the huts. When the battle ended, at least five or six hundred Pequot men, women and children lay dead.

Sassacus, hurrying with his remaining warriors from his second fort not far from the Thames, came too late to help. He was driven back by musket fire. A chase across most of southern Connecticut followed, until the Pequots were trapped in a swamp at Fairfield. Most of them were killed by colonial troops, and those who gave themselves up were sold as slaves in the West Indies, turned over to the Narragansets or to the less-than-tender mercy of Uncas. The mighty Pequot nation had been destroyed.

(Since this primarily involves Connecticut Indians, the Pequot War is covered in my *The Indian in Connecticut* in greater detail than possible here. C.W.)

THE COMING OF THE WORD

Both Pilgrims and Puritans, as we know, had announced the Christianization of the "sauvages" as one of their major objectives in coming to America. This perhaps stood secondary to gaining the freedom to practice their own brand of Christianity and to exploiting the vast resources of this new land, but certainly they wasted little time in getting to work on it.

For a time their conversions were few and strongly resisted by both sachems and powwows. Historians usually ascribe this to the Indians' fear that if Christianity were introduced, they would lose much of their power over their own people. No doubt this was a reason, but there probably was another and deeper one. These Algonkian peoples, as we have said before, already possessed a religion with many beautiful aspects. More than that, it was related to every facet of the lives they lived. Undoubtedly many of the wise men honestly felt that without that religion their whole way of life would lose its meaning. This is precisely what happened eventually with many Indians, although it cannot by any means be blamed entirely upon their Christianization.

Perhaps it was best said, a long time ago, by a sachem to a white man: "Our people bow to the sun when it rises in the morning. We can watch it on its journey across the sky. We know what it can do for us, and what it cannot do. Your people worship a god whom they cannot even see. You don't know what he can do and what he can't do. Which is the better way?"

Even Massasoit, that long-time loyal friend to the white men, voiced a complaint. In 1639 he came to Plymouth, accompanied by his eldest son, to renew his treaty of peace and friendship with the English. He begged them to insert a clause to prevent the proselytizing of the Indians by white ministers, but his request was refused. He signed the treaty but went away disappointed.

But of course, we can dismiss the complaint of Massasoit, if we prefer, with the words of the Reverend William Hubbard of Ipswich who declared that despite Massasoit's humanity to the English, ". . .he manifested no small displacency of spirit against them, as they were Christians." He tried to get the Pilgrims "never to attempt to draw any of his people from their old pagan superstitions and devilish idolatry, to the Christian religion . . . a bad omen. . . ."

The proselytizing continued and increased considerably with the arrival of "Praying" John Eliot in 1631. Teacher of the church at Roxbury, he, in Winthrop's words, "found such encouragement, as he took great pains to get their language, and in a few months could speak of the things of God to their understanding; and God prospered his endeavors, so as he kept a constant lecture to them in two places, one week at the wigwam of one Wabon, a new sachem near Watertown mill, and the other the next week in the wigwam of Cutshamekin near Dorchester mill . . . and the Indians began to repair thither from other parts. . . ." Eventually he translated the entire Bible into the Algonkian tongue.

In connection with this, it is said that one sachem, after being persuaded to read Eliot's Bible by a colonist, returned it with the wry comment: "That is a wonderful religion you have. Why don't you practice it?" John Eliot, however, did practice it, and there is no doubt as to his sincerity. Nor did it fail to have results.

Others followed in his footsteps, notably the Mayhews on Martha's Vineyard and Nantucket, and by 1674 at least 4000 had been converted. By 1651 the first "Praying Indian" town had been established at Natick, and bylaws were adopted with the aforementioned Wabon serving as justice of the peace. All town offices, in fact, were held by Indians. Nashobah Plantation (Littleton) was incorporated in 1654. By the time of King Philip's War in 1675, Eliot and his followers had established some 30 "Praying Indian" towns in the area.

It seems reasonable to assume that many, perhaps the great majority, of these conversions were genuine. It must also be noted that English authority and English justice seemed, in the eyes of many Indians, to be a constant threat, and it could pay to have such a man as John Eliot for a friend. Furthermore, as one Indian has recently suggested to me, these people saw the settlers crowding around them, their old way of life and their means of gaining a livelihood fast disappearing. They could and sometimes did go hungry. As friends and converts of John Eliot and his followers, they would, they believed, at least be fed.

All these conversions, plus the power demonstrated by the English in the Pequot War, brought a number of sachems to the Bay Colony and to Plymouth officials to offer their acknowledgments of and submission to the English rule. One, however, remained conspicuously aloof. This was Miantinomo of the Narragansets. He was not unfriendly, and he apparently did not object when some of his sannops went with Mason on his expedition against the Pequots, yet he seemed always to have been under suspicion.

In 1640 Winthrop wrote of a "rumor of the Indians plotting mischief against the English . . . that Miantinomo had sent great present of wampum to the Mohawks, to aid him against the English," that the present was "accepted, and aid promised." Governor Haynes of Connecticut was convinced of the truth of this rumor, but Governor Thomas Dudley of the Bay Colony and his council did not believe it. Nevertheless, they sent Captain Jenyson with three men and an Indian interpreter to the Narraganset sachem to "know the truth." They were "kindly entertained" by Miantinomo, but he refused to talk in the presence of their interpreter "because he was a Pequod, and a servant, and their enemy, and might discover their counsels." When the English produced an acceptable interpreter, Miantinomo denied the truth of the rumor and professed his friendship to the colonists. He would be willing to go to Boston as Captain Jenyson wished, if Roger Williams might come with him.

This request the captain denied him, but nevertheless Miantinomo did accede to Jenyson's request, was met at Dorchester by a guard, and according to Winthrop, "well entertained at Roxbury by the governor," but again the matter of a "Pequod" interpreter came up. The governor (Dudley) refused to use another, "thinking it a dishonor to us to give so much way to them. Whereupon he came from Roxbury to Boston, departing in a rude manner, without showing any respect or sign of thankfulness to the governor for his entertainment, whereof the governor informed the general court, and would show him no countenance, nor admit him to dine at our table, as formerly he had done, till he had acknowledged his failing, etc., which he readily did, as soon as he could be made to understand it, and did speak with our committees and us by a Pequod maid who could speak English perfectly.

"But it was conceived by some of the court that he kept back such things as he accounted secrets of state, and that he would carry home in his breast, as an injury, the strict terms he was put to both in this, and the satisfaction he was urged to for not observing our custom in matter of manners, for he told us that when our men came to him, they were permitted to use their own fashions, and so he expected the same liberty with us. So as he departed and nothing agreed, only the former articles of peace were read to him and allowed by him with this addition, that if any of his men did set traps in our jurisdiction, etc., they should be liable to satisfy all damages, etc." [Winthrop]

Again in 1642, Winthrop wrote that rumors went through the land, again by way of Connecticut and probably spread by Uncas and his Mohegans, "certifying us that the Indians all over the country had combined themselves to cut off all the English. . . ." To this the colonists first responded by taking away the arms of the Indians nearest to them, most of whom had long since demonstrated their friendship, and next by summoning Miantinomo once again, this time on the charge of drawing the rest of the Indians into a confederation against them.

> In all his answers he was very deliberate and showed good understanding in the principles of justice and equity. He demanded that his accusers might be brought forth, to the end, that if they could not make good what they had charged him with, they might suffer what he was worthy of, and must have expected, if he had been found

> guilty, viz., death. We answered, we knew them not, nor were they within our power, nor would we give credit to them, before we had given him knowledge of it, according to our agreement with him. He replied, if you do not give credit to it, why then did you disarm the Indians. . . .

He also accused Uncas of spreading these false reports, which was probably true. He further offered to meet Uncas at Boston at any time and "prove to his face his treachery." The English did nothing about this offer, but once again Miantinomo was cleared. At times one can only wonder if this "thorn in the flesh" of the English had not been self-imposed from the start. Miantinomo never was convicted of any serious wrongdoing, and it appears that his greatest crime in English eyes was his pride, his dignity, and his ability to reason with them almost as if he were their equal. The pride and dignity came naturally to a great Indian sachem, but the logic was Miantinomo's own.

Wrongly or rightly, the English, thanks to their friend Uncas the Mohegan, would soon find an opportunity to dispose of Miantinomo once and for all.

SEQUASSEN STIRS UP A STORM

In Connecticut, Sequassen, sachem of the River Tribes, had hoped that after the conquest of the Pequots under Sassacus he would regain his former influence in the area. Instead, he found Uncas riding high with as tyrannical a hand as any Pequot sachem. And what was even worse, Uncas had the backing of the English colonists.

Sequassen retaliated. His warriors killed a Mohegan, and made an attempt upon the life of Uncas. Uncas complained to the authorities at Hartford, and Governor Haynes attempted a reconciliation, but without success. Thereupon Uncas invaded Sequassen's territory, killed seven or eight of his men, wounded thirteen, burned his wigwams, "and carried away the booty."

Sequassen then called upon his kinsman and ally, Miantinomo, for help. In the words of Winthrop, Miantinomo "sent to Mr. Haynes to complain of Onkus. He answered that the English had no hand in it, nor would encourage them, etc." The Narraganset sachem, in accordance with the treaty he had signed in 1638, then sent a message both to Governor Haynes and Governor Winthrop, "and was very desirous to know if we would not be offended if he made war upon Onkus. Our governour answered, if Onkus had done him or his friends wrong and would not give satisfaction, we should leave him to take his own course." Haynes also answered, not quite so satisfactorily, but "promising to to be aiding to neither, etc."

Those replies, in the opinion of Miantinomo, gave him a free hand. Immediately he gathered together a large force, perhaps six or seven hundred warriors, and marched upon the Mohegan headquarters near present-day Norwich in Connecticut. Mohegan watchers spotted the Narragansets fording the Shetucket River, and rushed to warn Uncas in time for him to gather his own warriors. The two forces met face to face at a spot now called the Great Plain.

Uncas was not lacking in courage, but being considerably outnumbered, he resorted to trickery—a method in which he excelled. He asked for an interview with Miantinomo, and the two soon faced each other between the opposing forces. Uncas suggested that they settle the matter in single combat, the winner to gain control of the other's warriors, but Miantinomo refused.

"My men came to fight," he said, "and they shall fight."

Whereupon Uncas, expecting this answer, gave his prearranged signal. He threw himself flat upon the ground. His men, their bows already bent, loosed a shower of arrows upon the Narragansets. Uncas sprang up, and with his warriors yelling their battle cry and brandishing their tomahawks, rushed upon the astonished enemy.

Panic-stricken by the sudden attack, the Narragansets turned and fled! A chase followed over the countryside, and most of the fleeing warriors escaped, but Miantinomo wore a corselet given to him by the English, and this hampered his flight. He was finally brought to earth by a Mohegan sagamore named Tantaquigeon aided by another captain of the tribe. Soon Uncas came up and siezed him. Miantinomo sat down upon the ground, all but overcome with grief and shame. His own warriors had deserted him.

Uncas asked him why he did not beg for mercy. "If you had taken me," he said, "I would have besought you for my life."

Yet Uncas did not kill him. He was well aware that many of the colonists thought highly of Miantinomo. Despite his hatred of the Narraganset sachem, Uncas feared that killing Miantinomo might put he himself out of the good graces of the English. It was his friendship to the white men which had gained him most of the power he now held. Power, to Uncas, was more important than satisfying his hate.

The colonists of Rhode Island soon demanded Miantinomo's release, but Uncas ignored them. Instead, he took his captive to Hartford and asked the governor and council to decide the fate of Miantinomo.

Those authorities had a better idea. Only a few months before, in May of 1643, the two colonies of Massachusetts had joined with those of Hartford and New Haven to form the United Colonies of New England. (The Rhode Island colonies had not been invited to join.) Hartford decided to pass the responsibility on to the Commissioners of the Council, holding their first meeting in September, for final decision.

The Council members also preferred not to decide. They favored Uncas, but could find no sufficient cause for the death of Miantinomo. So they passed the troublesome problem on to a convention of fifty New England clergymen now meeting in Boston.

Five of the "most judicious elders" quickly made the decision. They returned the captive to Uncas for execution. Uncas took Miantinomo back to the scene of the battle, where the Mohegan's brother Wawequa came up behind him and drove a hatchet into Miantinomo's head.

According to Winthrop, the reasons for this decision were as follows:

> 1. It is now clearly discovered to us, that there was a general conspiracy among the Indians to cut off all the English, and that Miantunnomoh was the head and contriver of it.
>
> 2. He was of a turbulent and proud spirit, and would never be at rest.
>
> 3. Although he had promised us in open court to send the Pequod to Onkus, who had shot him in the arm with intent to have killed him, (which was by the procurement of Miantunnomoh as it did probably appear,) yet in his way homeward he killed him. He beat one of Pumham's men and took away his wampum, and then bid him go and complain to the Massachusetts [Colony].

Thus, Winthrop piously concludes, he had forfeited his life by the Indian customs, and by the fashions of all countries. Or rather, this was apparently the conclusion of the Commissioners of the United Colonies, in acting upon the decision of the clergy.

The above seems to rank high among the chronicles of self-justification after the fact. To take these items in order:

1. It never was "clearly discovered" that Miantinomo was the head of a "general conspiracy" or even that there was a general conspiracy. The whole thing may well have been a rumor, fashioned by Uncas to keep himself in the good

graces of the English. And in any case, Miantinomo had long since been cleared of this charge.

2. Yes, it appears that Miantinomo was of a proud and turbulent spirit.

3. The Pequot had attacked Uncas, then fled to Miantinomo for protection, about the only place he could find protection from Uncas. Miantinomo considered himself honor-bound not to turn the man back to Uncas for probable torture and certain execution, yet the authorities in Boston had forced him to agree to do so. Apparently one of his men, either with or without his direction, resolved the problem by killing the Pequot. As to the matter of Pumham's man, that was a tempest in a teapot for which Miantinomo perhaps deserved a slap on the wrist.

And regardless of Indian custom, as DeForest points out in his *History of the Indians of Connecticut,* it was hardly the custom among civilized nations, even at that time, to hold a man prisoner of war for weeks and then cold-bloodedly order his execution.

What it boils down to is that because of his "proud spirit," Miantinomo had to die.

Thus disappeared from the scene a most personable man, a man highly respected by many, and one who by his own standards at least was a just and honorable man.

SUBMISSION

It now appeared that the colonists had eliminated all possible threats to themselves. The Narragansets were forced by the English to make peace with the latter and all their allies, which of course included Massasoit and Uncas. They did so, much against their will, because they had no choice. And with the English apparently now firmly in control, further submissions of the tribes in Massachusetts poured in.

Nor did the English make submission a simple or easy matter, as Winthrop shows in the case of Pumham, sachem of Shawomock, and Sacononoco, sachem of Patuxet, who first were grilled concerning the Ten Commandments, in this fashion:

> 1. Quest. Whether they would worship the true God that made heaven and earth, and not blaspheme him? Ans. We desire to speak reverently of Englishman's God and not to speak evil of him, because we see the Englishman's God doth better for them than other Gods do for others.
>
> 2. That they should not swear falsely. Ans. We never knew what swearing or an oath was.
>
> 3. Not to do any unnecessary work on the Lord's day within the gates of proper towns. Ans. It is a small thing for us to rest on that day, for we have not much to do any day, and therefore we will forbear on that day.
>
> 4. To honor their parents and superiors. Ans. It is our custom to do so, for inferiors to be subject to superiors, for if we complain to the governor of the Massachusetts that we have wrong, if they tell us we lie, we shall willingly bear it.
>
> 5. Not to kill any man but upon just cause and just authority. Ans. It is good, and we desire to do so.
>
> 6. 7. Not to commit fornication, adultery, bestiality, etc. Ans. Though fornication and adultery be committed among us, yet we allow it not, but judge it evil, so the same we judge of stealing.
>
> 8. For lying, they say it is an evil, and shall not allow it.

> 9. Whether you will suffer your children to read God's word, that they may have knowledge of the true God and to worship him in his own way? Ans. As opportunity serveth by the English coming amongst us, we desire to learn their manners.

In addition to this, they were forced to appear before the governor and sign a form, which they did. And according to Winthrop, "they departed joyful and well satisfied. We looked at it as a fruit of our prayers, . . . and that the Lord was by this means making a way to bring them to civility; and so to conversion to the knowledge and embracing of the gospel in his due time."

Until that day should come, however, it appeared that the Indian was not quite a human being. At least, if we are to judge by the notation in Winthrop's *Journal* which appeared shortly thereafter:

"[July]5. There arose a sudden gust at N.W. so violent for half an hour, as it blew down multitude of trees. It lifted up their meeting house at Newbury, the people being in it. It darkened the air with dust, yet through God's great mercy *it did no hurt, but only killed one Indian* with the fall of a tree. It was straight between Linne and Hampton."

The italics, of course, are mine.

And the submission continued. In the following year Winthrop notes that "Cutshamekin and squaw sachem, Masconomoco, Nashacowam, and Wassamagoin, two sachems near the great hill to the west called Wachusett . . . desired to be received under our protection and government upon the same terms . . . and the court gave each of them a coat of two yards of cloth, and their dinner; and to them and their men every of them a cup of sack at their departure, so they took leave and went away very joyful."

It should be noted that the "Form of Submission" included an agreement by the sachems to "put ourselves, our subjects, lands and estates under the government and jurisdiction of the Massachusetts, to be governed and protected by them, according to their just laws and orders, so far as we shall be made capable of understanding them. . . ."

Thus peace for the most part prevailed, and according to Winthrop, by 1644 "all the sachems from Merrimack to

Tecticutt" (Taunton) had "tendered themselves to our government." Nevertheless in that same year Pessacus and Canonicus (still the sachem of the Narragansets, although he had by now grown quite old and Pessacus was largely acting in his stead, as Miantinomo had done) asked permission of the English to attack Uncas in revenge for the death of Miantinomo. Permission was refused, but Pessacus nevertheless crossed over with a sizeable force to Connecticut and attacked. He succeeded in trapping Uncas and his men within the Indians' Fort Shantok, and doubtless would have forced their surrender had not the English brought supplies up the river to them. Seeing the English present and not wanting to make war with them, the Narragansets retired.

In 1647 Canonicus died, a very old man. At some point thereafter Canonchet, son of Miantinomo, assumed his position as sachem of the Narraganset. In 1655 Edward Winslow of the Plymouth Colony, old and true friend to Massasoit, died. Massasoit realized that he was losing all his old friends among the English. He ordered his two eldest sons, Mooanam or Wamsutta and Metacomet or Pometacom, to go to Plymouth and adopt English names. It would appear that he thought of this as a means of protection, of making it easier for them to take their places in the English scheme of things.

At any rate, the magistrates were much impressed with the noble bearing of these two handsome young men. They gave them names right out of the heroic pages of Greek history: Alexander for the elder, Philip for the younger.

Then, in 1661, Massasoit abdicated his sachemship, left his base at Mount Hope and moved in with his old friends and allies, the Nipmucks. This somewhat scattered tribe ranged from areas around the present Worcester as far down as northeastern Connecticut, and apparently, based in the present town of Webster, around Lake Chargoggagoggmanchauggagoggchaubunagungamaugg. There today stands a sign reading: HOME OF THE NIPMUCK INDIANS.

This put Massasoit in territory very close to that claimed by Uncas, the Mohegan-Pequot sachem. The power and territorial claims of Uncas had expanded as his influence with the colonists increased. Now he attacked the Nipmucks.

Massasoit tried to intercede with the English, hoping they would force Uncas to make restitution for the damage he had caused. This attempt resulted in partial failure. It appears that Uncas received no more than a gentle slap on the wrist. This newer and more powerful friend, the colonists seemed to feel, was of more value than an old man who was no longer even Grand Sachem of the Wampanoag Federation.

In the following year Massasoit died. He was widely hailed among the colonists, and no doubt by some of the Indians as well, as a man of peace. One cannot help but suspect that he died a somewhat disappointed man. He had aided the Pilgrims—a small, virtually impoverished group of white men, with little knowledge of the ways of the wilderness, who would probably not have survived without his help. He had done this largely out of kindness and quite possibly in the knowledge that in the end this would strengthen his hand as grand sachem of his confederation. He had freely granted them large tracts of land, at a time when land seemed of little value in the thinly populated area. Throughout he remained steadfast in his own religious faith. Yet at the urging of John Eliot, he sent one of his younger sons to Harvard, that training school for Puritan divines.

With all his old friends dead and he himself aging and ill, he was given little help by the white men when he had tried to intervene for his friends the Nipmucks against the encroachments of Uncas. And even he must have realized that the aid he gave to one small group of Englishmen had helped to bring swarms of their countrymen to settle in their wake. Now they were crowding the coast and moving so far inland that there was hardly enough room left for the Indian to live the life to which he was accustomed.

Massasoit's son, incidentally, did not stay on in the new brick dormitory at Harvard to graduate. Only one of the four Indians sent there by Eliot did so. And though Massasoit did not live to see it, that son would die on the side of his people, fighting against the white men.

Alexander, the eldest once called Mooanam or Wamsutta, now reigned as undisputed Grand Sachem of the Wampanoag Federation.

AN END TO PEACE

It is doubtful that either Alexander or Philip entirely accepted their father's views. They had come too late upon the scene, and seen too much, to share his early optimism. They could see the wild land that was their livelihood disappearing under the strokes of the axe and the furrows of the plow. They could see Indians punished for breaking white men's laws which were contrary to their own sense of justice, or which they did not even understand. Perhaps they could even sense, behind the show of friendliness in their treatment by the magistrates, the thinly-veiled contempt in which they were held.

At any rate, Alexander had barely settled down to his sachemship before he was summoned to appear before the magistrates at Boston. Rumors had been flying thick and fast that Alexander was preparing for war upon the colonists, and this time they may have been true. Certainly he held the possibility in his mind, though he was far from ready for overt action. And it is said that he answered the summons in great fear.

Nevertheless, he gave a good accounting of himself to the authorities which seemed to satisfy them. They feasted him, and he started back on the homeward journey. But on the way a violent illness seized him and he died before he reached Mount Hope. Had the English poisoned his food? This appears unlikely, although not impossible. The important thing is that his younger brother Philip believed they had done so and would never be convinced otherwise.

That, to Philip, was the final blow in a long string of injustices. He inherited the sachemship from his brother at the age of twenty-four, and within a few years he had begun to plan for war.

From this distance in time, it is difficult to make an accurate estimate of Philip's character. Hubbard speaks of his "ambitious and haughty spirit," and adds such phrases as "this treacherous and perfidious caitiff," "the naughtiness of his own heart," his "cowardly temper and disposition" and "evil and malicious mind." He also calls him a "notorious traitor" and "a bloody wretch." But once even this somewhat prejudiced historian speaks of Philip as "that grand Rebel," which comes very close to being a term of admiration. Or perhaps the Reverend Hubbard meant in this sense to compare Philip with Satan, that rebellious angel.

In any event, most later historians tend to regard Philip in a much more favorable light. John W. DeForest, certainly a more careful researcher than Hubbard, spoke in the 1840s of Philip's "proud spirit of independence" and "heroism." Others have characterized him as an Indian patriot and statesman, though not a great leader in battle. These estimates seem to hold up well in the light of such facts as are available to us. There is little if any evidence of cowardice in Philip's actions, and a leader who rises up to fight a foreign power that has forced his people to subjection is generally regarded as a patriot rather than a traitor.

War did not break out for several years, and it is possible that Philip hoped the matter could be resolved eventually by peaceful means. He did succeed, when he reaffirmed the peace treaty made by his father some years before, in securing a promise from the colonists that no more Indian land would be bought for the next seven years. But within a year, white settlers were again taking over Indian territory. Philip, if he had ever hoped for peace, must now have abandoned that hope.

In fact, it is quite possible that he planned on war from the time of his brother's death, convinced that there was no alternative save eventual extinction. But he was no mean strategist and he knew that, outnumbered as the Indians were by the whites, he needed all the allies he could persuade to join him. A war under such circumstances of quick attacks, destruction, and fast retreat into the forest where he could be hidden by friends, was the only answer. Furthermore, it would require the hoarding of food and ammunition supplies against such a time as Indian villages, planting grounds and hunting areas might be controlled by the colonists.

Philip had a quick mind and an imposing presence, but apparently with the older sachems of the tribes he lacked some of the persuasiveness of his father. Still, it must not be forgotten that Massasoit had been able, at least in part, to strengthen the Wampanoag Confederation because he had the power and the friendship of the white men behind him. For example, the Cape Indians had willingly joined the confederation in Massasoit's time, but now, largely Christianized, they would take no part in a war against the white man. The sachems of the powerful Narraganset tribe were hesitant to battle with the English, although eventually they did join with Philip. Their cousins the Eastern Niantics, whose sachem was Ninigret, refused to do so. But the Nipmucks, and the Pocumtucks of Western Massachusetts, eventually went over to Philip's side.

Such careful preparation could not remain unnoticed by the colonists. Rivalries among tribes and sachems, always a weakening factor when Indians tried to form alliances against the whites, played their part. And there were always leaks, so that the rumors flew faster than ever, this time not without foundation. Philip was more than once ordered to Plymouth or Boston to give an accounting of his actions, and for the most part managed to give satisfactory answers to the white authorities.

Then, in 1671, he was summoned to Taunton and ordered to surrender the guns of his braves. He turned over his own weapon as did the seventy men who accompanied him. But when he went back to Mount Hope, the rest of the sannops under his jurisdiction refused to do likewise. He told the magistrates that he had not understood this to be expected of him. Perhaps this was true, and it may be that he did not try very hard, but in any case, if he had insisted it is likely that he would have been faced with open revolt amongst his own men. These men had obtained their guns in trade or as gifts; by now they had learned how to use them well in hunt and battle and they were not about to give them away with war looming ahead.

Philip went on making his plans, strengthening alliances wherever he could. Then Sassamon returned to the tribe. Sassamon had gone to Harvard and been converted to Christianity. Since then he had (or at least said he had) renounced that religion and wished to go back to the faith and the land of his fathers. Since he knew English well, he became Philip's secretary. Thus he learned of Philip's secret plans for war and promptly informed the English of them. The authorities summoned Philip to Plymouth, but nothing could be proved and he was released.

Shortly afterwards, Sassamon's body was found in a frozen pond. His hat and gun lay on the bank, so that it looked as if he might have fallen into the water or leaped in to die of his own accord.

This of course did not satisfy the colonists. They found bruises upon the body and "by a strange Providence" located an Indian who professed to have seen the killing. Promptly three Indians were arrested, one Tobias and his son, and one of Philip's councillors. Brought to trial in Plymouth, they were convicted upon very flimsy evidence. What proved the case against them according to the learned Dr. Increase Mather, was the fact that blood oozed from the body upon the approach of the accused, "as if it had been newly slain, albeit it was buried a considerable time before that." The councillor and Tobias were hanged, and the son was shot awhile later.

War, if it could have been averted earlier, was now inevitable. Both Roger Williams and Samuel Gorton—the latter especially scorned by Pilgrim and Puritan alike because of his distain of their religious beliefs—attempted to intervene but failed. Josiah Winslow, Governor of Plymouth Colony, wrote Philip asking for a pledge of peace. Philip's answer showed all the pride of a true king:

"Your governor is but a subject of King Charles. I shall not treat with a subject. I shall treat of peace only with the King, my brother. When he comes I am ready."

Actually, he would have preferred to wait a little longer. He had by now forged a strong alliance among the New England tribes, but not as strong as he wished it to be. The Narraganset were still reluctant to go to war, although some sources state that they had made a tentative agreement to join with Philip in the following year, 1676.

But Philip could no longer hold his braves in. They were ready for battle. Finally, on June 20, 1675, he allowed a party of them to raid the village of Swansea, not far from Mount Hope. They swarmed into the village and terrified the inhabitants, who fled to their garrison house. The Indians set fire to some of the dwelling houses and killed any cattle they found. But no one, neither colonist nor Indian, was killed or even seriously injured.

Then, three days later, a white man shot an Indian and the following day the Indians retaliated. Hidden in the woods, they fired upon a party returning from church, killing one man and wounding several others. Two more, on their way to get a surgeon, were likewise slain, along with six men killed at a dwelling house in the settlement.

The war was on. The Pocassets, ruled by the squaw sachem Weetamo, widow of Philip's brother Alexander and daughter of Corbitant, hurried north to join the fighting Pokanokuts. At some point, quite possibly later, the women and children of Philip's fighting braves were sent at his request to the Narraganset country for safety.

Meanwhile, the inhabitants of Swansea fled and sought help from the Massachusetts authorities at Boston. A party on horse and afoot, under the command of Captains Henchman and Prentice, marched in the direction of Mount Hope. Along with them was the company of one Samuel Mosely, a former privateer, whose company consisted of 110 volunteers, buccaneers of his own class, and several dogs. They were joined by Plymouth troops under Major Cutworth and Captain Benjamin Church. The latter would eventually become the colonists' hero of the war, a man even respected by his Indian enemies for his fair and honest dealings.

For the moment the colonists did not have much success. The Indians, it seemed, would not come out to take part in open combat, but "lay concealed or skulking about the garrison," and thus succeeded in killing a number of their white enemies. Eventually the colonists crossed onto the neck of Mount Hope and succeeded in clearing it of Indians. They found Philip's wigwam deserted. While the English foolishly paused to build a fort in this conquered territory, the grand sachem was continuing his devastations eastward, having planned in advance not to allow himself to be trapped on the Mount Hope peninsula.

By this time the Nipmucks and the Pocumtucks had come into the war, as well as a few tribes in Maine and New Hampshire. The English, still not trusting the faithful Cape tribes, insured their neutrality by seizing the tribes' women and holding them as hostages! Now the United Colonies, the two in Connecticut plus the colonies of Plymouth and Massachusetts Bay, proceeded to raise an army of about a thousand men. To these would soon be added Uncas and several of his Mohegan-Pequots, always ready to make war upon Wampanoag or Narraganset.

Nevertheless the devastation continued, sweeping northward and westward as far as the Connecticut River in Massachusetts and including the settlements at Springfield and Deerfield. In that area Philip himself was said to have appeared riding a black horse and leaping over fences, but it is possible that in their terrified state the colonists were imagining Philip in every Indian they saw.

The war continued for two years or more, and entire volumes have been written about it. But there is only room here to relate the more salient facts and results. In the course of the fighting more than half of Medfield was burned, Mendon abandoned and burned, and Middleborough destroyed. All the garrison houses in Rehoboth were razed, Marlborough was fired and Springfield demolished by fire. At Sudbury, near Green Hill, Philip ambushed colonial troops, killing 29 of them and setting fire to the woods. Only 14 escaped. Westport was devastated and Wrentham fired, but the inhabitants fled to Dedham. Acushnet was all but destroyed. The battle at Bloody Brook emptied the town of Deerfield, and for some years thereafter, the houses stood vacant. Groton and Lancaster were also devastated. In all, the Indians attacked 52 of the 90 towns of New England, destroying thirteen of them, and killing around 600 fighting men—about one out of every ten colonists of military age. And most of the ravaged towns of the frontier would not be occupied again for years.

SLAUGHTER IN THE SWAMP

As mentioned before, the Narraganset tribe at the start of the war was reluctant to join with Philip, a sachem of their long-time enemy, the Wampanoag Confederation. Furthermore, they had been forced by the English into an agreement to remain at peace and to turn over to the whites any of Philip's men who came to them for sanctuary. But since they had not made the agreement willingly, it was not considered binding and they did not keep it. They turned over no Wampanoag warriors to suffer white man's justice, and as the war continued, an increasingly large number of their sannops fought beside Philip.

The Narraganset had also complied with Philip's wish and taken the women and children of his warriors under their protection, hiding them in a fortified area in a swamp near Kingston, Rhode Island. But in December of 1675 one Peter, a renegade Narraganset, led a large force of the colonists to the hideaway. The English attacked on December 19, and according to Hubbard and most other historians, a bitter battle ensued. Of the more than a thousand white troops engaged (along with 150 of their Mohegan-Pequot allies) over 200 were killed or wounded. Finally they fought their way inside the stockade, and as Captain John Mason had done in Connecticut nearly forty years before, set fire to the huts. Thus several hundred women and children—and, according to the accounts of the historians, Narraganset warriors—were roasted alive.

Some, not all, of the Narraganset and Wampanoag people of today believe another account of all this—an account passed down from their ancestors in the Indian fashion. The account begins, as also related by historians, with Philip's request to a Narraganset to give sanctuary to his women and children. We shall assume, although we cannot know, that the Narraganset was Canonchet, their sachem.

Canonchet agreed to do so. "How about the old men?" he asked.

"No," Philip said. "The old men will stay with me and do the work of the women."

Thus, according to this account, the defenders of the fort who fought so bravely and effectively, but were later roasted to death in flames, consisted of only women and children!

Perhaps the truth lies somewhere between. Perhaps there were a few, but only a few, Narraganset braves left at the fort to protect the women and children. If so, and if the reports of the colonists on their own casualties are true, then those few braves exacted a heavy price for their lives.

Off Rhode Island Route 2, north and east of Charlestown, a road leads to the site of the Great Swamp Fight. There, on a rise of ground in the swamp, stands a tall monolith, with tablets around it commemorating the troops of the various colonies which took part in the fight. In September of 1972, Christian Narragansets held their annual memorial service for the warriors and women and children slaughtered there. But they also prayed for the souls of the white soldiers who died in the battle. And when Tall Oak, one tribesman who considers the affair of December 19, 1675 as not a battle but a massacre, attempted to protest this latter action he was not allowed to speak. Or at least, someone apparently unplugged his microphone. This in turn brought a strong letter of protest from the United American Indians of New England. Thus, three hundred years later, the matter is neither settled nor forgotten.

But the affair in the swamp did not by any means put an end to the war. Though the Narragansets were hunted and harassed in their homeland, they could still strike back, and now they were openly allied with Philip. Canonchet, brave as his father Miantinomo before him, swore that he would not surrender a Wampanoag nor the paring of a Wampanoag's nail. Time and again that winter he and Philip struck their enemies. They burned village after village, and either killed the inhabitants or forced them to flee through the snow. A hundred fighting men under Captains Pierce and Wadsworth were "swallowed up," as Hubbard puts it.

Then, in the spring, the tide began to turn. Necessity forced Canonchet and a party of his men to go back to their country to find corn for planting, for their people had spent a hungry winter. There they were set upon by a party of Connecticut troops and Mohegan-Pequot braves under Captain Denison, and Canonchet was captured. When Denison told him he would be put to death, Canonchet answered:

"It is well. I shall die before my heart is soft; before I have said anything unworthy of Canonchet to say."

He was taken to Stonington and shot. Denison's Indian allies beheaded and quartered his body, and Denison sent the head to the magistrates of Connecticut as a trophy.

In the following months, the colonists continued their attacks upon Canonchet's people, until they were all but driven from their own country. During the year, more than two hundred were killed.

Not long after this, Philip and his party, most of them Narragansets, attempted an escape back to Narraganset country. At the Taunton River, they were forced to fell a tree for crossing. There Captain Church and his company attacked them, but they escaped into the forest. They crossed the river at a ford farther on, hotly pursued by the English. There a number of the women and children were captured, among them Philip's wife, Wootonekanuske, and his nine-year-old son.

The chase grew hotter. A day or two later, Philip and his band were surprised while preparing breakfast, and 173 of them captured. Philip and a few of his principal chiefs escaped.

After that time, for Philip, one disaster followed upon another. His wife and son were prisoners, most of his allies had been defeated or had defected to the enemy. Some of his tribesmen denounced him and joined the English, to the point where his force dwindled to a handful of warriors. Weetamo, squaw-sachem of Pocasset, Philip's sister-in-law and faithful ally throughout the war, attempted with a few of her braves to escape across the Tehticut River into her

own country. They were surprised by a body of the colonial troops on the 6th of August and all captured except Weetamo. Later she was found dead near the river bank.

The colonials cut off her head and put it on a pole in Taunton. Her subjects, now captive there, burst into cries of grief at the sight. This, Mather called "a most horrid and diabolical lamentation."

Shortly thereafter Philip, desperate and despondent, fled with his few remaining warriors back to Mount Hope Neck. He sat there one evening in what was known as the King's Seat, high on a rock above the bay, conferring with two of his tribesmen named Alderman. One of the brothers, weary of the war, advised surrender or flight northward. Philip, it is said, flew into a rage and killed him.

The other Alderman brother left, vowing vengaence. He sought out Captain Church and his men, now in Rhode Island, and informed the captain where Philip could be found. The captain and his troops rode off at once.

Alderman told them where Philip had made camp, on a spot of dry land near the Mount. They crossed the bay in the night and approached the spot. Church, with one force, lay in ambush in the swamp, while Captain Golding surrounded the camp with another.

Early in the morning Golding's men opened fire. Philip and his men, taken completely by surprise and half-clothed, rushed at full speed into the swamp. Philip, in the lead, soon came within range of a colonist and Alderman. The soldier's gun misfired, but Alderman's bullet went to Philip's heart, and he fell upon his face in the swamp.

This happened on the morning of August 12, 1676. Church's Indians dragged Philip's body out of the mire and one of them beheaded and quartered it. His head was displayed for a long time in Plymouth, where a few years later the pious Mather, having gloated for a while over the skull, took out the jawbone of "that blasphemous leviathan" and made off with it.

Most of Philip's party managed to escape, led by an old sachem named Annawon, who had been a great warrior under Massasoit as well as Philip. Later in the month Church, with a small force, succeeded in capturing them. The Indians with the English troops had gone among them and convinced them of Church's kindness, so that most of them submitted quietly, giving up their arms. Annawon ordered his women to prepare supper for Church and his men, and they all supped in peace together.

Later in the evening Annawon went a short distance and returned to Church with Philip's regalia.

"Great captain," he said in English, "you have killed Philip and conquered his country, for I believe that I and my company are the last that war against the English, so suppose the war is ended by your means, and therefore these things belong to you." He gave to Church two broad belts worked in wampum, two horns of powder, and a red cloth blanket.

The two captains talked together through the night, and Annawon gave an account of what mighty success he had formerly in wars against many nations of Indians, when he served Asumequin (Massasoit), Philip's father. Church grew fond of the old warrior, and when he took him to Plymouth tried to intercede in his behalf with the authorities. Nevertheless, he was put to death. Tispaquin, the last of Philip's great captains had surrendered upon promise of mercy; he was executed at the same time as Annawon. Any Indian, in fact, who was believed to have taken part in the war suffered a like fate.

For the rest, slavery in the colonies or the Indies awaited them. Increase Mather wanted the nine-year-old son of Philip executed, but eventually he was sent in chains to Bermuda along with his mother. A group of about 160 peaceful Indians who lived in the Dartmouth area, but had taken no part in the attack upon and virtual destruction of that town, delivered themselves up to Captain Eels, "upon promises of good treatment." They were taken to Plymouth and, over the protests of both Eels and Church, sold as slaves and "transported to foreign parts."

Some fighting continued for more than a year in Maine and New Hampshire, but for the Indians of Massachusetts and Rhode Island the war was over. Nipmuck and Pocumtuck, and probably some of the Wampanoags and Narragansets, fled westward across the Hudson and northward as far as Canada, and may eventually have been absorbed there by their distant relatives, the Algonkians of Canada. Some of the Wampanoag group sought and were given sanctuary by their one-time allies, the Cape Indians. Probably Ninigret of the Eastern Niantics took a few of his cousins of the Narraganset tribe, while many went north to join the Abnaki or west to the Mahicans.

And what of the Praying Indians? Those on the Cape seem to have fared well enough and apparently their women were returned to them. The others did not fare so well. Philip had looked upon them as enemies—allies of the whites —and treated them accordingly. In most cases Philip was right, for few of them went over to his side. Nevertheless, the English suspected them of secretly doing so, and in far too many cases treated them as enemies. Even those who fought bravely and well as soldiers against their own people were afterward scorned and insulted by their one-time comrades-in-arms.

Probably the worst treatment of all was that accorded to the Naticks, who had been loyal from the beginning to their Christian teachers. In midwinter these residents of Wamesit (Tewksbury) were ordered to move to Long and Deer islands in Boston Harbor. They had neither shelter nor sufficient food. When John Eliot and a friend tried to take a boatload of supplies out to them, angry colonists tipped the boat over, leaving the two of them in the icy waters.

Eliot and his friend survived, but a great many Indians did not. In the spring Thomas Oliver brought the survivors, sick and half-starved, back to his land on the Charles River. A few struggled on to their homes, but in the end most of the Praying Towns had to be abandoned. By 1684 there were only four such towns left from thirty or more once built and settled. And even there, they no longer were allowed to hold town offices or take any part in their own government. Forced to live by white men's rules and governed by white men's laws, their lands stolen away by white men, they deteriorated rapidly.

Many historians believe that had Philip been able to keep his confederation together and had all the tribes of the area joined him in the war, the English colonies in Massachusetts might have been wiped out. Possibly true, but my own feeling is that Philip's attempt came too late. The time to have struck and won was (as Corbitant of Nemasket had then argued in council) when the one settled colony consisted of less than fifty men, women and children at Plymouth, already weakened by a winter of hardship. At that time Massasoit chose the way of peace, and so sealed the doom of Wampanoag and Narraganset alike.

Even then, wiping out that one small group might not have been enough. Others would certainly have come later to try again, as they did in Virginia when the first attempt failed. The promise of vast riches in this wild land was too much for the white man to resist.

THE STOCKBRIDGE INDIANS

One Indian tribe or confederation survived for some time in spite of white men's encroachments. This was the Mahican of western Massachusetts, whose people came in time to be known as the Housatonic or Stockbridge Indians. They were, as mentioned early in this book, largely a peaceful people, and had, according to their accounts, managed a treaty with the fierce Mohawks to the west, which defined the limits of Mohawk hunting grounds. Earlier, the Mohawks had apparently pushed them east of the Hudson.

In the early part of the eighteenth century the English colonists appear to have thought of the country west of the Connecticut River as a wilderness unbroken by white men. They made several settlements along that river but went no further. They were wrong in their conjecture. In the early 1720s, when they did travel as far as the Housatonic River in search of further lands to settle upon and till, they found several Dutchmen there already engaged in farming and trading. These people had fled as early as 1684 from the Dutch settlements along the Hudson to escape the virtual slavery of the patroon system.

They were getting on well with the Housatonic Indians. Although the English looked askance upon the Dutch, they also found the Indians very friendly. In the present southern Berkshire County area, there were but two settlements, both calling themselves *Muh-he-ka-neew (Muh-he-ka-ne-ok* in the plural), meaning "the people of the great waters continually in motion." One group, under Chief Konkapot, lived in what would later be known as the Great Meadow, in Stockbridge, just north of the brook which now bears the chief's name. The other group, under Umpachene, had their wigwams on the Housatonic in the northern part of the present Town of Sheffield, at a place called *Skatecook* (a variant spelling of Schaghticoke, "where the small stream empties into the large one and corn lands adjoin." The small stream in this case was the Green River.)

At one time, they said, they had numbered between them a thousand warriors. But by 1720 the two groups had hardly fifty people, including women and children. They had taken no part in King Philip's War, though it is recounted that in 1676 one Major Talcot "surprised and brought slaughter upon a body of fleeing Indians" in what is the present village of Great Barrington. This was supposedly somewhere in the vicinity of what the Mahicans called "the Great Wigwam," on the site of the present-day Congregational Church and not far above an Indian ford of the Housatonic. But these were probably fleeing Narragansets. (A note by Hubbard's printer says the battle was "probably" fought in Stockbridge.)

In 1724 the English colonists had already prepared the way for themselves. Chief Konkapot, journeying to Westfield with twenty other Indians, signed a treaty which opened most of southern Berkshire to them, including the present towns of Sheffield, Great Barrington, Mount Washington, Egremont, and most of Stockbridge, West Stockbridge and Lee, as well as a small part of Alford. And upon arrival in the area, the colonists soon found opportunity to increase their influence by opening the way for the Gospel. For they found Konkapot, the "principal man among them, was strictly temperate, a very just and upright man in his dealings, a man of prudence, and industrious in business, and disposed to embrace the Christian Religion."

Without delay, various influential reverend gentlemen laid the subject before the Board of Commissioners of Indian Affairs. Subsequently, Governor Belcher commissioned Konkapot a captain of militia and Umpachene a lieutenant and presented the matter to them when they went to Springfield to receive their commissions. The two chiefs approved it. This was followed by a full-scale conference with all the Mahicans at Housatonic. After four days they finally agreed to receive a religious teacher. Young John Sergeant, a Yale graduate and tutor, was given the job, and met with the Mahicans in October, 1734 at "Housatonnuk."

In two weeks, the Indians had put up a church and school in Great Barrington. The school opened in November, with 22 or 23 Indian children for scholars. Shortly thereafter Konkapot and Umpachene and their families, along with Ebenezer Poopoonah, who had been acting as interpreter for the whites, were baptized.

After that matters must have transpired so quickly as to leave the Mahicans breathless. The two groups had to be closer together, the English decided, for purposes of school and church. In 1736 they were granted a tract six miles square in Stockbridge in return for giving up their previous landholdings, and church and school were removed there. The Mahicans asked only that four of the Dutch settlers, whom they liked and who lived in the area granted to the Indians, be allowed to remain there. This request the colonists granted reluctantly. The Dutch, it seems, gave rum to the Indians, which actually was physically harmful to them. In addition this would make it difficult for the white men to thoroughly Christianize them.

Finally the English succeeded, in one fashion or another, in easing out these friendly Dutch and forcing them to move "below the mountain," but the Dutch presented other problems. It seemed that back in 1685 they had received Indian patents in "Westenhook." These patents included "a very large part of the Housatonic Valley in Berkshire" and even ran down into northern Connecticut—in other words, some of the same land that had now been purchased by the English from the Mahicans. This resulted in a series of lawsuits. Some of the Dutch were eventually dispossessed, but many remained and their descendants will be found in the area today.

Meanwhile Indian-white relations remained peaceful. After the Town of Stockbridge was incorporated in 1739, both Konkapot and Umpachene served on the original Board of Selectmen, and for several years thereafter the Board included one or more Mahicans. The new Mission House, built in 1739, still stands as a fine example of Colonial architecture, although moved from its first site to the village proper. Jonathan Edwards followed John Sergeant as the missionary minister.

In the wars with the French and Indians of Canada, which continued until 1763, the Berkshire settlers were spared most of the slaughter and holocaust which fell upon settlements along the Connecticut River—such as Deerfield, where Canadian Indians and French, under French command, massacred many of the inhabitants and carried most of the rest off to slavery. It is believed that the presence of the Mahicans in the area, few as they were, acted as a buffer against the enemy. Several of them, in fact, served with the colonial forces in these wars.

In the Revolutionary War, an entire company of the Stockbridge Indians was formed under the command of Captain Daniel Ninham. They acted often as scouts, but also fought as a company, and fought bravely and well against the forces of General Howe at the Battle of White Plains on October 28, 1776. Some were killed and several others wounded.

They had asked, when forming the company, that the Continental Congress "would devise some method to prevent them from getting too much strong drink." How well this request was honored is not known, but it is known that at the end of the war General Washington paid them by giving each a blanket!

During the sixty-odd years that the white man and Mahican lived side by side, there is only one recorded incident of violence between them. This happened near Tyringham in 1755, when two white men came upon an Indian sitting with his family by his campfire and promptly killed him for no apparent reason. Later the two white men were tried, one acquitted and the other lightly punished. Not long after, a group of white men, riding down a wooded trail nearby, were fired upon by Indians from ambush and two of them killed. That more or less evened the score, and nothing further on the matter is recounted. Nor is it said, or even suggested, that the Indians involved were Mahicans.

Nevertheless, by the time the Revolution ended, the Mahicans had had enough of living in a land surrounded by white men. They saw their young men corrupted by white man's ways and white man's liquor. They saw their way of life diminishing and they felt, justly or not, that they had been bilked of much of their land. There must have been other incidents, perhaps minor ones, involving conflict between

Indian and white man. At any rate, in 1783 they sent the following petition to the Commonwealth of Massachusetts:

> To the Senators and—men of the Commonwealth of Massachusetts who are about to smoke their Pipes together in doing the Great Business of the State—
>
> We the Chiefs of the Moheakonnuk Tribe of Indians residing in Stockbridge this day met together beg you to listen to us a few words—
>
> Brothers—We remember we were once Great, and you were Small when you first came on this Island but afterwards We became Small as you became Great, and now we are very small and you are very great. We also remember that our Forefathers have often looked to you for Protection, Advise and Assistance. We with Pleasure look back and consider you have always heard us, when we have Spoken to you. Now Brothers since we are small we look to you as Children to their Fathers. We wish you would always remember as Parents do their Children. Brothers, we will put you in mind that ever since we first see you, we were always true Friends to you in all the Wars, untill this present Day. In this late War we have suffered much, our Blood has been spilled with yours and many of our young men have fallen by the side of your warriors, almost all those Places where your Warriors have left their Bones there our Bones are seen also—now we who remain are become very poor. Now Brothers, we will let you know we have been invited by our Brothers the Oneidas to go and live with them. We have accepted their invitation.
>
> Brothers. We will now tell you what we desire of you. We wish you in your wisdom to make some Laws that will protect and gard us while we may remain or hereafter have occation to come into your Government. We wish you to appoint a few of our Neighbors, whom we believe to be our Friends, to have Power to take Care of the little Interest of Land We have in this Town, that have been appropriated to a public or private use, either to sell or lease it out for us as they and We shall think best, directing them also to confirm all such Lands as we have honestly sold. We

wish to have them described, carefully to examine into all our Bargains for Land that the White People have made with us and see that we hant been cheated and endeavor to do justly by us and by those who have bought of us and have not as yet had their Lands confirmed to them, that when we are ready to remove, We may feel well towards all our Neighbors. We wish only to reserve Power to ourselves to do a little Business as Proprietors with regard to some unappropriated Lands. We wish that the Purchasers of our Lands might pay these our Friends for their Trouble.

Brothers We will only ask one Thing more, that we might not be sued in the Law for any future Debts We may hereafter contract.

Stockbridge Sept 2, 1783

Johoiakim Motokson
Joseph Shaugushqueat
Hendrick Aupaumut
Jehoiakim Nau naph tonk
Joseph Quononikaut

The authorities of the Commonwealth—the "Brothers" to whom the Mahicans addressed their petition—eventually concluded that the Indians had no further claims to territories in the Berkshire area. In fact, they went so far as to declare that some of the lands now occupied by the whites had been paid for two or more times. They may have been right.

At any rate, the Mahicans made their move, and by 1789 the last of them had gone. But their stay at Oneida with the Brotherton group was not of long duration. White land speculators were busy, and they soon found themselves as crowded by white settlers as they had been in their old home. Their friends the Miamis invited them to move to land they owned along the Ohio. Along with the Munsees, they moved there—only to find that the land had already been sold to white men.

Their next move was to Wisconsin. A few went on from there to Indian lands in Oklahoma, but most stayed in Wisconsin. In the early 1830s they lived on the east side of Lake Winnebago, but that land soon proved too valuable, and eventually they were moved north to Shawano County, near the village of Bowler. There within the past year, in a rare move sponsored by Congressman Silvio Conte who represents Western Massachusetts, the U.S. Congress granted them an additional 13,000 acres of "agriculturally marginal" farmland!

There they live quite peacefully and in some apparent content. Most farm, but many have gone on to make their mark in medicine and other professions. The tribe still keeps in touch with Stockbridge, writing letters to Mrs. Polly Pierce, Curator of the Historical Room of the Stockbridge Library. Now and then, a few of them return for brief visits to the land of their fathers.

Otherwise, as far as Massachusetts is concerned, it may be said that the Mahicans have passed into history and are preserved only in artifacts. Many such artifacts have been unearthed over the years—axes, stone pestles (some of fine workmanship), and on rare occasions stone tomahawks. Many more will no doubt still be found. Some Indian burial grounds have been torn apart, but one is still preserved in Stockbridge and one in Sheffield. And of course there is still the Mission House.

Maus-waw-se-ki (Monument Mountain) still stands, on Route 7 between Great Barrington and Stockbridge, but there is not a great deal left of the monument which gave the mountain its name. This pile of stones, according to Chief Konkapot, marked the spot of the treaty limit with the Mohawks, and also the grave of a great sachem of the Mahicans, and each passing Indian added a stone to the pile. Now no Mahican is left to tend the sachem's grave.

NON-VANISHING AMERICANS

It might appear, from the historical accounts of the time, that after 1676 every Indian fled from Massachusetts and Rhode Island save the few Mahicans, and that after they left there were no Indians remaining in the two states. This of course is not true. In 1960, the U.S. Census showed 3,050 Indians in the area. The Census of 1970 showed 4,475 in Massachusetts, 1,390 in Rhode Island, for a total of 5,865—almost double that of ten years before! Very probably not many of these are pure-blooded Indian. Usually, there was a grandparent or great-grandparent or great-great-grandparent who was English or Portuguese or Cape Verdean or African, but these increasing numbers are nonetheless proud to consider themselves Indians.

In the case of the Pocumtucks, it is probably true that they are gone. Throughout the early 1600s, this aggressive confederacy had fought white man and Indian alike, and particularly the Mohegan under Uncas. Finally, in 1664, they murdered a Mohawk ambassador. The retaliation of the Mohawks was so fierce and so thorough that the Pocumtucks were all but destroyed. There were still enough warriors left to play a noticeable part against the colonists in King Philip's War, but after that the survivors, too few to form even a tribe, much less a confederation, fled westward to Scaticook on the Hudson and eventually northward to join the St. Francis Indians in Quebec.

Furthermore, the remnants of the tribes belonging to the Massachuset Confederation, nearly devastated by plagues and war with the Abnakis to the north, had long since sought shelter with other tribes and so lost their identity.

But the Nipmuck had by no means vanished into the north for good. One authoritative source states that most of the seven Christianized villages followed King Philip and after the war fled westward or to Canada. If so, the Hassanamiscos of Hassanamesit (Grafton) must have been an exception. Princess White Flower, the present head of her tribe, advises me that her people have always lived there. Being herself engaged in preparing an extensive history of her family, tribe and area, she has a perfectly simple and logical answer to the puzzle. She states that, "Many of the men left or were taken away during the war but many women and children stayed behind."

This is probably the answer in the case of some of the other tribes as well. Certainly their men had no choice but to flee or be destroyed, even if they had not actually fought beside Philip. As previous examples have shown, the victorious, vengeful and still shaken colonists were then wasting little time in determining a man's guilt or innocence, as long as he was an Indian.

The Hassanamisco, incidentally, formed the second of the Praying Bands set up under the aegis of the Reverend John Eliot. The Naticks were the first, and the Nipmucks as a whole formed the majority of these Praying Bands. The Hassanamisco group included James the Printer, who attended Cambridge School and assisted Eliot in translating and printing the first Indian Bible. Princess White Flower (Zara Ciscoe Brough) is a descendant of James the Printer.

At any rate, by 1728 there were still (or again) enough Nipmucks in the Grafton area to cause the Commonwealth to set aside 7500 acres as a reservation for them, which included the site of the village of Hassanamesit (a place of many small stones). As in so many cases, the reservation has since been whittled down to less than 12 acres, but this small area includes the original Longhouse, built in 1590. Perhaps even more important, since 1962 a replica Longhouse Museum has been constructed which contains life-size figures of the Indians with their crafts and other implements. The old Printer/Ciscoe Longhouse has an Indian/Colonial Research Library and files containing data on 200 Indian tribes. The entire complex is dedicated to the Eastern American Indian and is open to the public by appointment from May 1st to October 1st. In addition, an Indian fair and pageant is held annually on the July 4th weekend, and is open to the public. Sure to be present are some of the approximately 400 Nipmucks scattered about the United States today.

Remnants of various other tribes live in Plymouth and Norfolk counties, but the Wampanoag as a confederation, for all practical purposes, came to an end when Philip died. Nevertheless, Chief Mittark (Lorenzo Jeffers) bears the title of Supreme Sachem of the Wampanoags, and a number of Indians classify themselves as Wampanoag, rather than by the use of their original tribal name, such as Pokanokut. Many of the survivors of this tribe, as well as of other tribes which fought in the war, in the end took refuge with their friends and one-time allies on Cape Cod.

The Indians of Gay Head, once members of the confederation, now number about 200. In 1711, because they were Christianized, the Society for Propagating the Gospel acquired land on Martha's Vineyard for them (land they originally owned). They still hold it, even owning a small town. They fish, make pottery and beadwork, and some of the men are fine artists. The Mashpee of Cape Cod are also fairly numerous, having communities at Mashpee, Yarmouth and Waquoit.

The Narraganset (people of the small point) tribe, supposedly wiped out by King Philip's War, has also survived. We know some were taken in by their cousins, the Eastern Niantics, who had taken no part in the war. Others apparently joined with the Mahican or the Abnaki of Maine or went on to Canada and never came back. Quite possibly, as with the Nipmuck, these were only the warriors, not the women and children. There are at least 500 in Rhode Island today and some estimates run as high as a thousand. Most of them live in the vicinity of Charlestown, but there is a second group to the north in Providence County. Two miles from Charlestown, they celebrate Rhode Island Indian Day on a Saturday in August with colorful and ancient ceremonies. On the following day services are held at the old Indian church on the grounds, followed by further tribal ceremonies. All this is open to the public, as is the annual powwow held earlier in the summer at Lafayette, Rhode Island. There is also an October Festival and the aforementioned observance of the Great Swamp Fight.

History sometimes has a way of ignoring Indians when they are not fighting with whites, but we do know a little about these Indians. Many fought in the American Revolution, alongside the descendants of the one-time enemies of their people. And where they perhaps excelled most of all was aboard the whaling ships when that industry was at its height in the nineteenth century. They proved to be fine seamen, and the hardships of a long voyage that took them far from home did not trouble them.

As an example of their seamanship, they tell on the Cape of a time many years ago when a passenger vessel out of Boston ran aground on a rock ledge off Martha's Vineyard. The sea was so rough that the Coast Guard deemed rescue impossible. But the Gay Head Indians, whalers all, did not. They put out in their own dory, made several trips through the stormy waters, and got every passenger and crewman safely ashore.

Some of these Indian whalers in time became harpooners, a position requiring great skill. But never, it seemed, no matter how great their ability, could they rise to the rank of captain. I have found one instance, perhaps the only one, where an Indian rose to chief mate. Even then, he was discriminated against. When one whaling vessel met with another, it was customary for the captain and the chief mate of one to be invited aboard the other to wine and dine. But in this case, the captain never took his Indian mate along with him!

The problem of the New England Indian throughout the years has been much the same problem he met with as a whaler. Having no other choice, he had to live as the white man lived, but it always seemed that he had to be much better than the white man to rise to an equal level. Some have made it in spite of the odds—rising high in the professions, as teachers, artists, nurses. There is Wamsutta (Frank James), Director of Music of the Cape Code Regional School at Eastham, and there is Helen Attaquin, a Gay Header and descendant of Massasoit, who is a university teacher, author, concert violinist and on her way to her doctorate in Education at Boston University. Others are excellent craftsmen, stonemasons and the like. Nor should it be forgotten that much of the high steel work in the Boston area has been done by Indians, men who are not afraid to walk a foot-wide beam hundreds of feet in the air.

Certainly the Indians of Massachusetts and Rhode Island are more than ever aware of their ancient heritage, and more determined to maintain it insofar as this can be done. The various gatherings, or powwows, held regularly in the area, with their tribal ceremonies, their Indian songs and Indian dances, may be only a good show to the watching whites, but to the Indian they help to keep alive the traditions of their people and perhaps their hopes for the future.

Just as Indians of different tribes, speaking the same root language but with a different dialect, found it difficult to converse with one another, so has it always been difficult for them to work together. It was that which made it comparatively easy for the colonists, using the "divide and conquer" system of the British empire-builders, to gain ascendancy. Today the Indians, despite their individuality and inevitable frictions, are slowly learning to work together. There is evidence of this in such institutions as the Multi-Service Indian Center at Dorchester, Massachusetts. Here Indians help other Indians to find jobs or to train for jobs and to adjust themselves to living in metropolitan Boston. There is also the Greater-Lowell Indian Cultural Association, presided over by Edward J. Guillemette.

Furthermore, the Indians of this area are demanding to be heard and making themselves heard. Perhaps most notable or at least newsworthy is the project begun by the Federation of Eastern Indians League, under the leadership of its president, Frank James. The League might be described as a nonviolent but militant Indian organization—militant, that is, in the sense of outspoken and unafraid. Thanksgiving Day, that day when the Wampanoag first brought food and dined with the Pilgrims, has been declared a National Day of Mourning by the Indians. On November 26, 1970, a sizeable group of them appeared at Plymouth, where white citizens, tourists and many local people in Pilgrim costume, were preparing to celebrate the 350th anniversary of the Landing and the first Thanksgiving.

These Indians came from all over the country, and the

majority were young. They brought shovels and promptly began to shovel sand upon the sacred Plymouth Rock! Hoping to avoid an open incident, the caretakers started to sweep off the sand with brooms.

"You may as well give up, white men!" the young Indians shouted. "You have to quit work at four-thirty. We can go on all night!"

Later, having covered the rock with several inches of sand, the young men departed for the replica of the *Mayflower,* which now lies in the harbor. A handful of them went up the ratlines and brought down the English colors under which the original ship had sailed. They also tossed a Pilgrim dummy overboard. The ship was eventually cleared by the local police without arrests.

"We are not here to cause trouble," Frank James said, "but we need to call the white man's attention to our problems and . . . we need to do it nonviolently."

The ceremony has been repeated in succeeding years. In addition, on Thanksgiving Day in 1972, a Day of Mourning ceremony was held in Washington, D.C., backed by Tall Oak, who is vice-president of the Federation of Eastern Indians League. There have, of course, been some incidents, and in at least one or two cases the Indians have taken the matter to court, but thus far there has been no open violence. Perhaps these events are doing what Frank James hoped they would—calling the white man's attention to the problems of the Indian—problems largely brought into being by the whites. It would do no harm for the white man to pause long enough to learn of these problems, of the desire of the Indian to live peacefully and prosper among them, yet to retain and be proud of his heritage.

After all, we do owe the Indians of this area something. It could even be said that we owe them New England.

BIBLIOGRAPHY AND SUGGESTED READING

The American Heritage Book of Indians, by the editors of *American Heritage,* with narrative by William Brandon: American Heritage Publishing Company, Inc., 1961.

Armstrong, W.C., *The Life and Adventures of Captain John Smith:* H. Dayton, N.Y., 1860.

Bonfanti, Leo, and the staff of *New England Journeys Magazine, Biographies and Legends of the New England Indians,* Volumes I, II and III: Pride Publications, Inc., Wakefield, Mass., 1969, 1970, 1972. Good material on all of the Noteworthy Indians of the area.

Bradford, William, *Of Plimoth Plantation,* (or *Bradford's Journal,) 1602-1646:* Boston, 1898 (first printing, 1856).

Brennan, Louis A., *American Dawn:* Macmillan, 1970.

Brennan, Louis A., *No Stone Unturned:* Random House, 1959.

Brownell, Charles DeWolf, *The Indian Races of North and South America;* Hurlbut, Kellogg & Co., Hartford, Conn., 1860.

Davidson, J.N., *A History of the Stockbridge Indians:* Silas Chapman, Milwaukee, 1893.

DeForest, John W., *History of the Indians of Connecticut:* First published in 1851 and since republished, with a biographical introduction, 1964, under the copyright of The Shoe String Press, Inc. of Hamden, Conn.

Hubbard, William (Minister of Ipswich), *A Narrative of the Indian Wars in New-England,* 1607-1677: Heman Willard, Stockbridge, Mass., 1803.

Indians of the Eastern Seaboard: U.S. Government Printing Office, 1967.

Massachusetts, A Guide to the Pilgrim State, Edited by Ray Bearse: Second Edition, Revised, Houghton Mifflin Co., Boston, 1971.

Morton, Thomas, *The New England Canaan:* London, 1637.

Mourt's Relation, A Journal of the Pilgrims at Plymouth: 1622; latest edition by Corinth Books, New York, 1963.

One Big Unhappy Family, by Robert Miller and Yema Nickel: *Yankee* Magazine, April 1973.

Underhill, Ruth M., *Red Man's Religion:* University of Chicago Press, 1965.

Vaughan, Alden T., *New England Frontier Puritans and Indians, 1620-1675:* Little Brown and Co., 1965.

Verrill, A. Hyatt, *The American Indian:* D. Appleton and Co., 1927 and 1943.

Vogel, Virgil J., *This Country Was Ours (A Documentary History of the American Indian):* Harper & Row, Inc., 1972.

Western Massachusetts, A History, Vols. I and II: Lewis Historical Publishing Company, Inc., New York and Chicago, 1926.

Willison, George F., *Saints and Strangers:* Reynal Hitchcock, New York, 1965.

Winslow, Edward, *Good News from New England:* London, 1624 (from Collections of the Massachusetts Historical Society, Vol. VIII, Boston, 1802.)

Winthrop, John, *History of New England, 1630-1649* (or *Winthrop's Journal*): Scribners, 1908; Barnes & Noble, 1959.

Wissler, Clark, *Indians of the United States:* Doubleday & Co., 1940; republished in 1966 by the same company in a revised edition prepared by Lucy Wales Kluckhohn.

Young, William R., Associate and Curator of Anthropology andArchaeology of the Springfield (Mass.) Museum of Science, Editor, *An Introduction to the Archaeology and History of the Connecticut Valley Indian,* published by the Museum in 1969. For anyone wishing to follow the trail of the ancient Indian, this will prove both fascinating and useful.

In the Historical Collection of the Stockbridge, Massachusetts Library:

Historical Memoirs Relating to the Stockbridge Indians, by Reverend Samuel Hopkins: S. Kneeland, Boston, 1753; reprinted by William Abbitt, New York, 1911.

Jones, Miss Electa F., *Stockbridge, Past and Present:* Samuel Bowles & Co., Springfield, 1854.

Observations on the Language of the Muhhekaneew Indians, by Jonathan Edwards, D.D.: Printed by Josiah Meigs, New-Haven, 1788.

INDEX